AF366952

Medical Credentialing Specialist

\-

The Comprehensive Guide

by

VIRUTI SHIVAN

Masters in Clinical Psychology (Major)

"In books, as in life, it's not the size or looks but the content that matters."

Introduction

Welcome to "Medical Credentialing Specialist - The Comprehensive Guide," a pivotal resource for those embarking on or advancing within the field of medical credentialing. This guide serves as your beacon through the intricate world of healthcare credentialing, ensuring you possess the knowledge, skills, and insights required to excel in this crucial sector of the healthcare industry.

The Essence of Medical Credentialing

At its core, medical credentialing is the backbone of healthcare quality and safety, serving as the gateway through which practitioners are vetted and validated to provide care. This process safeguards patients by ensuring that healthcare providers meet established standards of education, training, and competency. As a medical credentialing specialist, you are the custodian of this gate, tasked with a responsibility that is both significant and rewarding.

The Guide's Purpose and Approach

This guide is designed not only to introduce you to the fundamental aspects of the credentialing process but also to deepen your understanding of its implications within the healthcare system. Through this comprehensive exploration, we aim to equip you with the tools and wisdom needed to navigate the complexities of medical credentialing with confidence and proficiency.

Throughout the chapters, we delve into the intricacies of the credentialing process, legal and ethical considerations, the impact of technology, and the nuances of credentialing across various healthcare settings. Moreover, we provide insights into the interaction with insurance companies, continuing education, and the future of medical credentialing. Each chapter is enriched with hypothetical scenarios and personal anecdotes, bringing to life the challenges and triumphs that define this field.

The Unique Structure of This Guide

Structured to facilitate both learning and application, this guide is divided into chapters that meticulously cover every facet of medical credentialing. Each chapter includes detailed subchapters, culminating in exercises designed to test your understanding and apply your knowledge practically. Notably, this guide abstains from including images or illustrations for copyright reasons, focusing instead on rich, descriptive text that engages and informs.

As you progress through this guide, remember that your role as a medical credentialing specialist is not just administrative but pivotal to maintaining the integrity and quality of healthcare delivery. The insights and knowledge you gain here will serve as a solid foundation for your journey in this vital profession.

Conclusion

Embarking on this journey will challenge you to think critically, act ethically, and innovate within your role. The path of a medical credentialing specialist is both demanding and rewarding, filled with opportunities to make a significant impact on the quality of healthcare. As you turn the pages, engage with the content, reflect on the scenarios, and challenge yourself with the exercises, you are stepping into a role that is critical to the health and well-being of society.

Let this guide be your companion and mentor as you navigate the rewarding path of medical credentialing. Together, we will explore the depths of this field, uncover its challenges, celebrate its successes, and prepare for its future. Welcome to your journey as a medical credentialing specialist.

Chapter 1: The Role of a Medical Credentialing Specialist

1.1. Understanding Medical Credentialing

Medical Credentialing: A Definition

Medical credentialing is a systematic approach to verifying the qualifications and professional standing of healthcare providers. This process is essential for ensuring that practitioners who deliver care meet all the required educational, training, and licensure standards. It's the first line of defense in safeguarding patient safety and upholding the quality of care within healthcare facilities.

The Credentialing Specialist's Role

As a medical credentialing specialist, you play a pivotal role in this critical process. Your responsibilities include gathering, verifying, and assessing the credentials of healthcare providers to ensure compliance with national and institutional standards. This task involves a meticulous review of a practitioner's educational background, residency, licenses, certifications, and any other relevant qualifications.

Why Credentialing Matters

Credentialing is more than just an administrative hurdle; it's a vital component of healthcare administration that directly impacts patient care quality and safety. By thoroughly vetting the qualifications of healthcare providers, credentialing specialists help prevent unqualified individuals from practicing, thereby reducing the risk of medical errors and enhancing patient outcomes.

The Process at a Glance

The credentialing process typically involves several key steps:

- **Initial Application:** Healthcare providers submit detailed information about their qualifications, including education, training, and work history.

- **Verification:** Credentialing specialists verify this information by contacting universities, licensing boards, and previous employers.

- **Assessment:** Once verified, the credentials are assessed against the healthcare facility's standards or those set by accrediting bodies.

- **Decision:** Based on the assessment, a decision is made regarding the provider's eligibility to practice within the facility.

Challenges and Rewards

The role of a medical credentialing specialist is both challenging and rewarding. It requires a keen eye for detail, a high level of organization, and a deep understanding of healthcare regulations and standards. Specialists must navigate complex documentation and interact with a variety of institutions and individuals to verify credentials accurately.

Despite the challenges, the work of a credentialing specialist is immensely rewarding. By ensuring that only qualified and competent professionals provide care, specialists contribute significantly to patient safety and the overall quality of healthcare services.

Personal Anecdote

Imagine a scenario where an experienced credentialing specialist, Alex, identifies discrepancies in the application of a highly recommended surgeon. By diligently following up, Alex discovers that the surgeon's certification from a particular specialty board had lapsed. This discovery prompts a review and update of the surgeon's qualifications, ensuring that all practitioners at the facility are fully compliant with current standards. This example underscores the critical role of credentialing specialists in maintaining high standards of care.

Conclusion

Understanding medical credentialing is fundamental for those entering or currently within the field of healthcare administration. As a medical credentialing specialist, your role is crucial in maintaining the integrity and safety of healthcare delivery. Through your dedication and expertise, you ensure that the healthcare professionals who care for patients are qualified, competent, and up to the task. This Chapter sets the stage for a deeper exploration of the credentialing specialist's responsibilities, challenges, and impact on the healthcare system.

1.2. Key Responsibilities and Duties

The Core of Credentialing Work

The role of a medical credentialing specialist encompasses a broad range of responsibilities and duties, each critical to the effective verification and management of healthcare providers' credentials. This section outlines the key tasks that define the specialist's role, highlighting the importance of each in maintaining the standards of healthcare services.

Primary Responsibilities

- **Verification of Credentials:** The cornerstone of a credentialing specialist's duties is to verify the authenticity of healthcare providers' credentials. This includes checking educational backgrounds, training records, licensure, board certifications, and work history. Specialists use various sources, including direct communication with issuing institutions, to ensure all information is accurate and up-to-date.

- **Maintenance of Provider Records:** Credentialing specialists are responsible for maintaining comprehensive and current records for each healthcare provider. This involves updating documents as new information becomes available, such as renewed licenses or additional certifications, and ensuring that all records are secure yet accessible when needed.

- **Compliance with Regulations:** Healthcare facilities must adhere to numerous regulations and standards set by government bodies and accreditation organizations. Credentialing specialists ensure that provider credentials meet these requirements, thereby maintaining the facility's compliance and eligibility for insurance reimbursements and other critical aspects of healthcare operations.

- **Coordination with Healthcare Providers:** Specialists often serve as the primary point of contact for healthcare providers going through the credentialing process. This involves guiding providers through the application, addressing their queries, and ensuring they understand the requirements and timelines.

- **Liaison with Other Departments:** Credentialing specialists work closely with other departments, such as human resources and medical billing, to share relevant information about providers' credentialing status. This coordination is crucial for facilitating smooth onboarding processes and accurate billing.

- **Credentialing Committee Support:** In many organizations, a credentialing committee makes the final decision on a provider's eligibility to practice. Specialists prepare and present credentialing files to this committee, providing all necessary information to support informed decision-making.

- **Continuous Education:** Given the ever-evolving nature of healthcare regulations and standards, credentialing specialists must continually update their knowledge and skills. This involves attending workshops, seminars, and other educational opportunities to stay abreast of new developments in the field.

Hypothetical Scenario

Consider the case of Maria, a credentialing specialist who noticed an unusual gap in a new physician's work history. By following up with detailed inquiries and contacting previous employers, Maria uncovered that the physician had taken a year off for advanced training, which was not initially mentioned in the application. This diligence not only ensured the accuracy of the physician's credentials but also highlighted the importance of thorough verification in maintaining high standards of care.

Conclusion

The responsibilities and duties of a medical credentialing specialist are both varied and vital. Through their meticulous work, specialists ensure that healthcare providers meet the highest standards of professionalism and competence. This, in turn, directly contributes to the quality and safety of patient care. As the healthcare landscape continues to evolve, the role of credentialing specialists will remain indispensable, requiring ongoing dedication, precision, and a commitment to excellence.

1.3. The Importance of Accuracy and Detail

In the realm of medical credentialing, the importance of accuracy and detail cannot be overstated. Every document reviewed, every verification made, and every decision taken by a credentialing specialist has far-reaching implications on patient safety, healthcare quality, and the reputation of healthcare facilities. This section delves into why meticulous attention to detail is not just beneficial but essential in the credentialing process.

Accuracy: The Bedrock of Patient Safety

Accuracy in medical credentialing ensures that healthcare providers have the requisite training, experience, and qualifications to offer safe and effective care. A single oversight can lead to the accreditation of an unqualified provider, posing significant risks to patient health and safety. For instance, verifying the authenticity of a medical degree, licensure, and specialty certifications ensures that a healthcare provider is competent in their field of practice. This diligence is crucial in specialized areas of medicine where the skills and knowledge required are highly specific and directly impact patient outcomes.

The Role of Detail in Upholding Quality

The quality of healthcare services is directly tied to the qualifications and competencies of the providers. Credentialing specialists, by focusing on the minutiae of each credential, uphold these quality standards. This involves not just verifying that documents are genuine, but also ensuring that they meet the current standards and regulations of healthcare practice. For example, ensuring that a provider's continuing education credits are up to date reinforces a commitment to lifelong learning and adherence to the latest best practices in patient care.

Preventing Legal and Financial Repercussions

Inaccuracies in the credentialing process can have legal and financial consequences for healthcare facilities. If a provider whose credentials were not properly vetted is involved in a malpractice lawsuit, the facility could face legal action for negligent credentialing. Moreover, inaccuracies can lead to billing and accreditation issues, impacting the facility's financial health and its ability to provide services. This underscores the necessity for credentialing specialists to meticulously document and verify every piece of information.

Maintaining Reputation and Trust

The reputation of a healthcare facility hinges on the quality and reliability of its care. This reputation is built on the trust that patients and the community place in the facility's commitment to high standards. Credentialing specialists play a key role in maintaining this trust by ensuring that all healthcare providers in the facility are properly credentialed. This not only safeguards the facility's standing in the healthcare community but also reinforces public confidence in its services.

A Case for Diligence

Consider the scenario of a credentialing specialist who uncovers a discrepancy in the work history of a prospective provider. By taking the initiative to investigate further, the specialist may reveal gaps in practice that need explanation or additional training that wasn't initially disclosed. Such diligence ensures that only those truly qualified are entrusted with patient care.

Conclusion

The emphasis on accuracy and detail in medical credentialing is a testament to its critical role in safeguarding patient safety, ensuring the quality of care, and protecting healthcare facilities from legal and financial risks. Credentialing specialists, through their meticulous work, lay the foundation for a healthcare environment where excellence in patient care is the norm. Their commitment to precision is a cornerstone of trust in the healthcare system, making their role indispensable in the pursuit of outstanding healthcare delivery.

1.4. Exercise: 10 MCQs with Answers at the End

Multiple Choice Questions

1. What is the primary purpose of medical credentialing?

   - A) To increase the hospital's revenue

   - B) To verify the qualifications and professional standing of healthcare providers

   - C) To simplify the hiring process

- D) To create a database of healthcare workers

2. Which of the following is NOT typically verified during the credentialing process?

   - A) Educational background

   - B) Favorite color

   - C) Licensure

   - D) Board certifications

3. Who is responsible for conducting the credentialing process?

   - A) Medical assistants

   - B) Credentialing specialists

   - C) Nurses

   - D) Patients

4. Why is credentialing considered a critical component of healthcare administration?

   - A) It ensures all staff get along well.

   - B) It prevents unqualified individuals from practicing.

   - C) It guarantees high salaries for doctors.

   - D) It makes the administrative process longer.

5. What is the first step in the credentialing process?

   - A) Verifying board certifications

   - B) Assessing the provider's eligibility

   - C) Initial application by the healthcare provider

   - D) Decision making regarding the provider's practice eligibility

6. Which organization might a credentialing specialist contact to verify a physician's medical school education?

   - A) The local gym

   - B) The American Medical Association (AMA)

   - C) A previous employer

   - D) The medical school the physician attended

7. What might a credentialing specialist discover that could impact a provider's eligibility to practice?

   - A) A lapse in certification

   - B) The provider's preference for electronic health records

   - C) The provider's vacation plans

   - D) The color of the provider's medical school

8. The credentialing process is directly linked to which of the following outcomes?

   - A) Increased administrative paperwork

   - B) Enhanced patient safety and quality of care

   - C) Decreased healthcare costs

   - D) Simplified healthcare laws

9. What key skill is crucial for a credentialing specialist to possess?

   - A) Ability to fly

   - B) Keen eye for detail

   - C) Talent in drawing

   - D) Proficiency in cooking

10. How does credentialing contribute to the healthcare system?

   - A) By ensuring healthcare providers meet educational and professional standards

   - B) By organizing team-building activities

   - C) By promoting healthcare providers based on seniority

   - D) By reducing the need for medical insurance

Answers

1. B) To verify the qualifications and professional standing of healthcare providers

2. B) Favorite color

3. B) Credentialing specialists

4. B) It prevents unqualified individuals from practicing.

5. C) Initial application by the healthcare provider

6. D) The medical school the physician attended

7. A) A lapse in certification

8. B) Enhanced patient safety and quality of care

9. B) Keen eye for detail

10. A) By ensuring healthcare providers meet educational and professional standards

These questions and answers are designed to test your understanding of the medical credentialing process and the role of credentialing specialists in ensuring the quality and safety of healthcare services.

Chapter 2: The Credentialing Process

2.1. Steps in the Credentialing Process

The credentialing process is a systematic approach to ensuring that healthcare providers are qualified and competent to deliver care. This meticulous procedure involves several critical steps, each designed to verify different aspects of a provider's qualifications and background. Understanding these steps is essential for credentialing specialists, healthcare administrators, and anyone involved in maintaining the standards of healthcare delivery.

Initial Application

The credentialing journey begins with the **Initial Application**. In this phase, healthcare providers submit comprehensive information about their educational background, training, work history, and any certifications or licenses they hold. This information forms the basis of the credentialing process, providing a snapshot of the provider's professional qualifications.

Primary Source Verification

Following the application, the process moves into **Primary Source Verification**. This crucial step involves verifying the accuracy of the information provided by the applicant directly from the original source. Credentialing specialists contact educational institutions, licensing boards, and certification agencies to confirm each element of the provider's credentials. This step ensures that all claims about qualifications, licensure, and certifications are accurate and current.

Committee Review

Once verification is complete, the provider's application and supporting documents are presented to a **Credentialing Committee**. This committee, typically comprising healthcare professionals and administrators, reviews the verified credentials against the healthcare facility's standards. The committee considers the provider's qualifications, professional conduct, and any disciplinary actions in their history.

Onboarding and Privileging

Successful passage through the committee review leads to **Onboarding and Privileging**. Onboarding involves integrating the provider into the healthcare facility's systems and processes, while privileging is the process of granting the provider permission to perform specific procedures or services based on their credentials, training, and experience. Privileging is highly specific and is tailored to the provider's qualifications and the facility's needs.

Ongoing Monitoring and Re-credentialing

Credentialing does not end with onboarding and privileging. **Ongoing Monitoring and Re-credentialing** ensure that providers maintain their qualifications and adhere to professional standards. This phase includes regular checks on licensure, certification renewals, and monitoring of professional conduct. Typically, re-credentialing occurs every two to three years, requiring providers to undergo a similar process to ensure their credentials remain current and valid.

Personal Anecdote

Consider the story of Mia, a credentialing specialist who meticulously navigated a complex credentialing case. A foreign-trained physician applied to practice in a rural clinic. Mia's thorough verification process uncovered discrepancies in the translation of the physician's documents. By collaborating with the physician and a certified translator, Mia ensured the accurate representation of the physician's qualifications, ultimately facilitating the physician's successful credentialing. This example highlights the importance of diligence and attention to detail in each step of the credentialing process.

Conclusion

The credentialing process is foundational to maintaining high standards of care in healthcare facilities. Each step, from the initial application to ongoing monitoring, serves to ensure that healthcare providers are qualified, competent, and up to date in their field. For credentialing specialists, understanding and effectively navigating this process are crucial in upholding the quality and safety of patient care.

2.2. Verification of Documents and Credentials

The Pillar of the Credentialing Process: Verification

Verification of documents and credentials stands as the cornerstone of the credentialing process. This critical step ensures that the information provided by healthcare providers regarding their qualifications, such as education, training, licensure, and board certification, is authentic and current. The integrity of the credentialing process hinges on the meticulous verification of these documents, underscoring the credentialing specialist's role in safeguarding patient safety and healthcare quality.

Primary Source Verification Explained

Primary Source Verification (PSV) is the gold standard in the verification process. PSV requires obtaining confirmation of a provider's credentials directly from the original issuing source. This means contacting educational institutions for degrees, state licensing boards for licenses, and certification boards for board certifications. The aim is to validate the accuracy of the credentials claimed by the healthcare provider, ensuring they are not only genuine but also current and in good standing.

Techniques and Tools for Effective Verification

Credentialing specialists utilize a variety of techniques and tools to conduct effective verifications. These include:

- **Direct Contact:** Making direct inquiries to issuing institutions and boards via phone, mail, or secure online portals designed for credential verification.

- **Professional Credentialing Services:** Leveraging third-party services specialized in credential verification can streamline the process, ensuring thorough and timely verification.

- **Online Databases and Verification Systems:** Utilizing national databases such as the National Practitioner Data Bank (NPDB) for disciplinary actions and the American Board of Medical Specialties (ABMS) for board certification statuses.

Challenges in Verification

The verification process can present several challenges, including:

- **Inaccurate or Outdated Information:** Providers may inadvertently provide incorrect information, or their credentials may have lapsed without their realization.

- **Language Barriers and International Credentials:** Verifying credentials from foreign institutions can be complex due to language barriers and differences in educational or licensure standards.

- **Delays in Response:** Slow responses from institutions or boards can delay the credentialing process, impacting provider onboarding and facility staffing.

Strategies for Overcoming Challenges

Credentialing specialists employ various strategies to navigate these challenges, such as:

- **Establishing Clear Communication:** Ensuring that requests for verification are clear, concise, and contain all necessary information to facilitate a prompt response.

- **Building Relationships with Key Contacts:** Developing relationships with contacts at educational institutions, licensing boards, and certification agencies can improve response times and cooperation.

- **Staying Informed of International Credentialing Practices:** Gaining knowledge of international credentialing standards and practices helps in accurately assessing foreign-trained providers' qualifications.

Personal Anecdote

Imagine a scenario where Jordan, a seasoned credentialing specialist, encountered a challenging case involving a physician with credentials from multiple countries. Jordan's expertise in international credentialing practices, combined with his persistence in communicating with foreign institutions, ensured the accurate verification of the physician's qualifications. This diligence not only facilitated the physician's smooth credentialing but also underscored the significance of adaptability and resourcefulness in overcoming verification challenges.

Conclusion

Verification of documents and credentials is a fundamental aspect of the credentialing process, requiring a high level of diligence, accuracy, and attention to detail. Credentialing specialists play a critical role in this process, employing various techniques and strategies to overcome challenges and ensure the integrity of healthcare services. Through their efforts, credentialing specialists contribute significantly to maintaining the standards of excellence in patient care and safety within the healthcare system.

2.3. Working with Certification Boards and Licensing Agencies

The Crucial Alliance

Working with certification boards and licensing agencies is an indispensable part of the credentialing process for healthcare providers. These organizations are the gatekeepers of professional standards in the healthcare industry, ensuring that practitioners meet the requisite qualifications and maintain professional conduct. Credentialing specialists must navigate these relationships with expertise and diplomacy to verify the credentials of healthcare providers accurately.

Understanding Certification Boards

Certification boards are specialized entities that validate the qualifications and competencies of healthcare professionals in specific fields. For example, the American Board of Internal Medicine certifies physicians who meet rigorous standards in internal medicine and its subspecialties. Credentialing specialists must understand the certification criteria and processes of these boards to accurately assess a provider's qualifications.

Licensing Agencies: Gatekeepers of Practice

Licensing agencies, typically state-based, grant licenses to healthcare providers, allowing them to practice in a particular jurisdiction. These agencies ensure that providers meet state-specific educational, examination, and ethical standards. Credentialing specialists work closely with these agencies to verify the licensure status of healthcare providers, an essential step in safeguarding patient safety.

The Verification Process

The process of working with these entities involves several key steps:

- **Request for Verification:** Credentialing specialists submit formal requests to certification boards and licensing agencies to verify the credentials of healthcare providers. This request includes the provider's consent for the release of information.

- **Documentation Review:** Upon receiving the request, these entities provide documentation or official statements confirming the provider's certification or licensure status. The credentialing specialist reviews these documents for authenticity and accuracy.

- **Ongoing Communication:** Effective communication is crucial. Credentialing specialists may need to follow up on pending verifications or clarify discrepancies. Establishing a good rapport with contacts at these organizations can facilitate smoother verification processes.

Challenges and Solutions

Working with these entities can present challenges, such as delays in response times or discrepancies in records. Credentialing specialists can mitigate these challenges through proactive communication, maintaining detailed records of all interactions, and employing patience and persistence in following up on verification requests.

A Real-world Scenario

Imagine a scenario where a credentialing specialist, Jake, is verifying the credentials of a new provider, Dr. Lee. Dr. Lee has recently moved states and needs a new state license. Jake facilitates this process by liaising between Dr. Lee and the state licensing agency, helping to expedite the licensing process by ensuring all documentation is in order and submitted promptly. This collaboration not only helps Dr. Lee begin practicing sooner but also demonstrates the vital role of credentialing specialists in bridging the gap between healthcare providers and regulatory entities.

Conclusion

The relationship between credentialing specialists and certification boards and licensing agencies is fundamental to the integrity of the healthcare system. Through diligent verification of documents and credentials, credentialing specialists ensure that healthcare providers meet the highest standards of professional practice. This collaboration ultimately contributes to the delivery of safe, high-quality healthcare services.

2.4. Exercise: 10 MCQs with Answers at the End

Multiple Choice Questions

1. What is the primary purpose of working with certification boards and licensing agencies in the credentialing process?

  - A) To ensure healthcare providers have valid parking permits

  - B) To verify the qualifications and licenses of healthcare providers

  - C) To negotiate salaries for healthcare providers

  - D) To organize team-building activities for healthcare staff

2. Certification boards are responsible for:

   - A) Providing parking spaces to healthcare providers

   - B) Certifying healthcare providers in specific specialties

   - C) Offering culinary classes to healthcare providers

   - D) Managing healthcare facilities

3. Licensing agencies grant:

   - A) Licenses to pets owned by healthcare providers

   - B) Licenses allowing healthcare providers to practice in a specific jurisdiction

   - C) Permission to healthcare providers to sell medical equipment

   - D) Certificates for computer programming to healthcare providers

4. A formal request sent to certification boards and licensing agencies to verify a provider's credentials typically includes:

   - A) A gift basket

   - B) The provider's consent for the release of information

   - C) A promotional brochure about the healthcare facility

   - D) A request for a personal meeting with the board members

5. When discrepancies in records are found, credentialing specialists should:

- A) Ignore them

- B) Report the provider to law enforcement

- C) Follow up to clarify and resolve the discrepancies

- D) Automatically disqualify the provider from the credentialing process

6. Effective communication with certification boards and licensing agencies is crucial for:

- A) Planning holiday parties

- B) Facilitating smoother verification processes

- C) Gossiping about healthcare providers

- D) Selling healthcare products

7. Challenges in working with these entities may include:

- A) Delays in response times

- B) Too many holiday greetings

- C) Overabundance of parking spaces

- D) Excessive compliments

8. The verification process involves reviewing documents for:

   - A) Artistic content

   - B) Authenticity and accuracy

   - C) Humorous content

   - D) Spelling mistakes only

9. Proactive communication and detailed record-keeping are strategies to:

   - A) Increase confusion in the credentialing process

   - B) Mitigate challenges when working with certification boards and licensing agencies

   - C) Discourage healthcare providers from applying

   - D) Promote a new healthcare facility

10. Credentialing specialists bridge the gap between healthcare providers and regulatory entities by:

   - A) Ignoring state regulations

   - B) Facilitating the credentialing and licensing process

   - C) Hosting weekly parties

   - D) Focusing solely on administrative tasks

Answers

1. B) To verify the qualifications and licenses of healthcare providers

2. B) Certifying healthcare providers in specific specialties

3. B) Licenses allowing healthcare providers to practice in a specific jurisdiction

4. B) The provider's consent for the release of information

5. C) Follow up to clarify and resolve the discrepancies

6. B) Facilitating smoother verification processes

7. A) Delays in response times

8. B) Authenticity and accuracy

9. B) Mitigate challenges when working with certification boards and licensing agencies

10. B) Facilitating the credentialing and licensing process

These questions are designed to reinforce your understanding of the role and responsibilities of credentialing specialists, particularly in their interactions with certification boards and licensing agencies.

Chapter 3: Legal and Ethical Considerations

3.1. Compliance with Healthcare Laws

The Bedrock of Healthcare Practice

Compliance with healthcare laws is the cornerstone of ethical and legal practice within the healthcare industry. For medical credentialing specialists, understanding and adhering to these laws is paramount. These laws govern the licensure, certification, and privileging of healthcare providers, ensuring that only qualified individuals deliver care. They protect patients from harm, uphold the integrity of the healthcare system, and guide the operations of healthcare facilities.

Key Healthcare Laws and Regulations

Several key laws and regulations are crucial for credentialing specialists:

- **Health Insurance Portability and Accountability Act (HIPAA):** Ensures the protection of patient information. Credentialing specialists must ensure that any exchange of personal health information complies with HIPAA guidelines to protect patient privacy.

- **The Joint Commission Standards:** These standards focus on improving healthcare quality and patient safety. Credentialing processes must align with these standards to ensure healthcare providers are competent and facilities remain accredited.

- **State Medical Practice Acts:** Each state has its own set of laws governing the practice of medicine within its jurisdiction. These acts define the requirements for licensure, the scope of practice, and disciplinary actions for non-compliance.

Ensuring Compliance in Credentialing

Credentialing specialists play a critical role in ensuring compliance through:

- **Diligent Verification:** By thoroughly verifying the credentials, licensure, and certification of healthcare providers, credentialing specialists ensure compliance with state and federal regulations.

- **Regular Education and Training:** Staying informed about changes in healthcare laws and regulations is essential. Credentialing specialists must engage in ongoing education and training to remain compliant.

- **Documentation and Record-Keeping:** Maintaining detailed and accurate records of the credentialing process is vital for legal compliance. These records serve as evidence of due diligence in the event of an audit or legal scrutiny.

Ethical Considerations

Beyond legal compliance, ethical considerations are integral to the credentialing process. Credentialing specialists must navigate conflicts of interest, ensure fairness in the evaluation of credentials, and maintain confidentiality throughout the process. Ethical practices foster trust within the healthcare system and contribute to the overall quality of patient care.

A Practical Scenario

Consider a scenario where a credentialing specialist, David, discovers that a highly recommended surgeon's licensure is under review due to malpractice allegations in another state. Despite pressures to expedite the credentialing process due to the surgeon's reputation, David upholds legal and ethical standards by pausing the process until the review is complete. This decision, guided by a commitment to compliance and ethical practice, underscores the specialist's role in safeguarding patient safety and the integrity of the healthcare system.

Conclusion

Compliance with healthcare laws is not just a legal requirement; it's a moral imperative that ensures the safety and well-being of patients. Credentialing specialists are at the forefront of this effort, tasked with the critical responsibility of ensuring that healthcare providers meet the highest standards of practice. Through diligent verification, ongoing education, and ethical decision-making, credentialing specialists play a key role in upholding the legal and moral fabric of the healthcare system.

3.2. Ethical Standards in Credentialing

Foundations of Ethical Credentialing

Ethical standards in credentialing form the backbone of trust and integrity within the healthcare system. These standards guide credentialing specialists in conducting their duties with honesty, fairness, and respect for confidentiality. Adhering to ethical principles ensures that the credentialing process is impartial, transparent, and focused on safeguarding patient care.

Core Ethical Principles

Several core principles underpin ethical behavior in the credentialing process:

- **Integrity:** Credentialing specialists must handle all procedures and documentation with honesty and integrity, ensuring that all actions are transparent and accountable.

- **Fairness:** It's imperative to treat all healthcare providers equally during the credentialing process, without bias or favoritism based on personal relationships, reputation, or external pressures.

- **Confidentiality:** Protecting the privacy of healthcare providers' sensitive information is crucial. Credentialing specialists must ensure that personal and professional data are handled securely and disclosed only when necessary and appropriate.

Challenges and Ethical Dilemmas

Credentialing specialists may face ethical dilemmas, such as encountering incomplete or questionable information in a provider's application. Deciding how to proceed requires a careful balance between thorough investigation and respect for the provider's reputation and privacy. Additionally, potential conflicts of interest, such as credentialing a colleague or family member, must be managed with strict adherence to ethical guidelines.

Implementing Ethical Practices

To uphold ethical standards, healthcare organizations and credentialing departments should:

- **Develop and Enforce Clear Policies:** Establish comprehensive policies that define ethical practices and procedures in credentialing. These policies should address confidentiality, conflict of interest, and the equitable treatment of all applications.

- **Provide Training:** Regular training sessions for credentialing staff on ethical issues can help reinforce the importance of ethics in their work and update them on best practices and legal requirements.

- **Establish a Review Board:** An ethics review board can offer guidance on complex ethical issues and review the credentialing process to ensure ethical standards are being met.

Real-World Application

Imagine a scenario where a credentialing specialist, Sarah, uncovers evidence suggesting that a physician may have falsified part of their credentialing application. Sarah faces an ethical dilemma: how to investigate further without unjustly damaging the physician's reputation. Guided by ethical standards, she confidentially escalates the issue to the ethics review board, ensuring a fair and thorough investigation that protects both the integrity of the process and the rights of the individual.

Conclusion

Ethical standards are the cornerstone of the credentialing process, ensuring that it is conducted with integrity, fairness, and respect for confidentiality. By adhering to these principles, credentialing specialists play a vital role in maintaining the trust and safety of the healthcare system. Ethical challenges require careful navigation, but with clear policies, training, and the support of an ethics review board, credentialing specialists can uphold the highest ethical standards in their crucial work.

3.3. Handling Sensitive Information

Essentiality of Confidentiality

In the realm of medical credentialing, the handling of sensitive information is a critical responsibility. Credentialing specialists are entrusted with vast amounts of personal and professional data about healthcare providers. This information, if mishandled, can have serious implications for privacy breaches and the integrity of the credentialing process. Therefore, understanding and implementing stringent measures to protect this data is paramount.

Principles of Data Protection

Protecting sensitive information involves adhering to several key principles:

- **Privacy:** Ensuring that personal information is accessed only by those who need it for the credentialing process and is not disclosed to unauthorized parties.

- **Security:** Implementing robust security measures, both physical and digital, to safeguard information from theft, loss, or unauthorized access.

- **Confidentiality:** Maintaining the confidentiality of information by handling it discreetly and according to legal and ethical standards.

Best Practices for Handling Sensitive Information

Credentialing specialists can adopt various best practices to ensure the security and confidentiality of sensitive data:

- **Secure Storage:** Physical documents should be stored in locked filing cabinets, and digital data should be protected with encryption and secure passwords. Access to these data should be restricted to authorized personnel only.

- **Data Minimization:** Collect only the information necessary for the credentialing process to minimize the risk associated with data handling.

- **Regular Audits:** Conduct regular audits of data storage and handling practices to ensure compliance with privacy laws and identify potential vulnerabilities.

- **Training and Awareness:** Regular training sessions for all staff involved in the credentialing process can help reinforce the importance of data protection and update them on the latest security practices.

Legal Compliance

Compliance with laws such as the Health Insurance Portability and Accountability Act (HIPAA) in the United States is crucial for protecting sensitive information. These laws provide guidelines for the collection, storage, and sharing of personal health information, and non-compliance can result in severe penalties.

Ethical Considerations

Beyond legal compliance, ethical considerations demand that credentialing specialists handle sensitive information with the utmost care. This includes respecting the privacy of healthcare providers and ensuring that their information is used solely for the purpose of credentialing.

A Scenario of Ethical Handling

Consider a scenario where a credentialing specialist, Michael, discovers an error in a physician's application that could potentially embarrass the physician if made public. Michael handles the situation ethically by discreetly contacting the physician to correct the error, ensuring the information remains confidential and the integrity of the physician is protected.

Conclusion

Handling sensitive information with care is a cornerstone of the medical credentialing process. By adhering to principles of privacy, security, and confidentiality, and by implementing best practices for data protection, credentialing specialists ensure the integrity of the credentialing process and safeguard the trust placed in them by healthcare providers and the institutions they serve. Compliance with legal and ethical standards is not just a regulatory requirement but a moral obligation to protect the professionals at the heart of healthcare delivery.

3.4. Exercise: 10 MCQs with Answers at the End

Multiple Choice Questions

1. What is the primary goal of handling sensitive information in the medical credentialing process?

   - A) To speed up the credentialing process

   - B) To ensure compliance with legal and ethical standards

   - C) To create a public database of healthcare providers

   - D) To facilitate marketing strategies

2. Which law is specifically designed to protect patient health information in the United States?

   - A) GDPR

   - B) COPPA

   - C) HIPAA

   - D) FERPA

3. The principle of **confidentiality** in handling sensitive information ensures that:

   - A) Information is accessible to everyone in the healthcare facility

- B) Data is stored in an unsecured location

- C) Information is disclosed only to authorized individuals

- D) All documents are digitized without any security measures

4. What type of security measures should be implemented to protect digital sensitive information?

- A) Encryption and secure passwords

- B) Public Wi-Fi networks

- C) Simple, easy-to-guess passwords

- D) Storing all data on a single, unsecured server

5. **Data minimization** in the context of sensitive information handling means:

- A) Collecting as much information as possible

- B) Collecting only the information necessary for the credentialing process

- C) Sharing all collected data with third parties

- D) Deleting all data immediately after collection

6. Regular **audits** of data storage and handling practices help to:

- A) Increase the workload unnecessarily

- B) Identify potential vulnerabilities and ensure compliance

- C) Share data with external entities

- D) Complicate the credentialing process

7. Training and awareness programs for staff involved in credentialing should focus on:

 - A) The importance of data protection and updates on security practices

 - B) How to use data for personal gain

 - C) Avoiding responsibility for data breaches

 - D) The best ways to share sensitive information on social media

8. Which of the following is NOT a principle of data protection?

 - A) Privacy

 - B) Security

 - C) Publicity

 - D) Confidentiality

9. Legal compliance in handling sensitive information ensures:

 - A) Credentialing specialists can avoid responsibility

 - B) The credentialing process is unnecessarily delayed

 - C) Protection against privacy breaches and adherence to laws

 - D) Information is shared freely with anyone interested

10. Ethical handling of sensitive information in medical credentialing requires:

   - A) Ignoring errors in a physician's application

   - B) Discreetly addressing errors and protecting the physician's integrity

   - C) Publicizing any discrepancies found in applications

   - D) Using sensitive information for marketing purposes

Answers

1. B) To ensure compliance with legal and ethical standards

2. C) HIPAA

3. C) Information is disclosed only to authorized individuals

4. A) Encryption and secure passwords

5. B) Collecting only the information necessary for the credentialing process

6. B) Identify potential vulnerabilities and ensure compliance

7. A) The importance of data protection and updates on security practices

8. C) Publicity

9. C) Protection against privacy breaches and adherence to laws

10. B) Discreetly addressing errors and protecting the physician's integrity

These questions are designed to reinforce the importance of handling sensitive information with care, ensuring legal compliance, and adhering to ethical standards in the medical credentialing process.

Chapter 4: Technology in Medical Credentialing

4.1. Software and Tools for Credentialing Specialists

The Role of Technology in Streamlining the Credentialing Process

In the evolving landscape of healthcare, technology plays a pivotal role in streamlining the credentialing process. Credentialing specialists leverage various software and tools to enhance efficiency, accuracy, and security. These technological solutions facilitate the management of large volumes of data, automate routine tasks, and improve communication and verification processes.

Key Software and Tools

- **Credentialing Management Systems:** These comprehensive platforms support every aspect of the credentialing process, from initial application to ongoing monitoring and re-credentialing. Features often include automated alerts for expiring documents, digital document storage, and integration with primary source verification databases.

- **Document Management Systems:** Specialized software for managing digital documents, including scanning, indexing, and secure storage solutions. These systems ensure that all necessary documentation is readily available and secure.

- **Verification Tools:** Online services and databases that provide instant verification of licenses, certifications, and other credentials. These tools significantly reduce the time and effort required for primary source verification.

- **Communication Platforms:** Secure email and messaging systems tailored for healthcare settings. These platforms ensure confidential and efficient communication among credentialing staff, healthcare providers, and verification sources.

- **Data Security Solutions:** Software solutions focused on protecting sensitive information, including encryption tools, secure data transfer protocols, and cybersecurity training programs for staff.

Benefits of Using Technology in Credentialing

- **Efficiency:** Automation of repetitive tasks frees up credentialing specialists to focus on more complex aspects of the credentialing process.

- **Accuracy:** Digital tools minimize human error in data entry and document management, leading to more accurate credentialing outcomes.

- **Security:** Advanced security measures protect sensitive information from unauthorized access or breaches, ensuring compliance with legal standards like HIPAA.

- **Scalability:** Technology allows credentialing processes to adapt and scale with the growth of healthcare facilities, accommodating an increasing number of providers without sacrificing quality or speed.

Considerations When Choosing Technology Solutions

- **Compliance:** Any technology used must comply with healthcare regulations and standards, particularly concerning data protection.

- **Integration:** Solutions should seamlessly integrate with existing systems within the healthcare facility, such as electronic medical records (EMR) systems.

- **Usability:** User-friendly interfaces and robust support services ensure that staff can effectively utilize the technology.

- **Customization:** The ability to customize features and workflows to fit the specific needs of the healthcare facility and its credentialing process.

A Real-World Application

Imagine a scenario where a healthcare facility transitions from a manual to a digital credentialing process. The facility adopts a credentialing management system that automates application tracking, document verification, and notification of credential expirations. This transition results in a significant reduction in processing times, fewer errors, and enhanced compliance with accreditation standards. Credentialing specialists, now able to manage their workload more effectively, can focus on ensuring the quality and integrity of the credentialing process.

Conclusion

The integration of technology into the medical credentialing process offers numerous benefits, from improved efficiency and accuracy to enhanced security. By carefully selecting and implementing the right software and tools, credentialing specialists can significantly improve the credentialing process, ensuring that healthcare providers meet the highest standards of care and compliance.

4.2. The Role of Data Management

Central to Credentialing Efficiency and Accuracy

Data management is a critical component of the medical credentialing process, playing a pivotal role in ensuring the efficiency, accuracy, and integrity of the entire operation. The role of data management in credentialing involves the systematic collection, storage, verification, and utilization of data related to healthcare providers' qualifications, licenses, and professional history. Effective data management strategies empower credentialing specialists to make informed decisions, maintain compliance with healthcare regulations, and uphold the highest standards of patient care.

Key Aspects of Data Management in Credentialing

- **Collection and Organization:** The first step involves collecting comprehensive data from healthcare providers, including educational backgrounds, licensure, certifications, and work history. Organizing this data in a structured, accessible format is essential for efficient processing and review.

- **Verification:** Data management systems facilitate the verification process by integrating with primary source verification tools and databases. This integration allows for real-time verification of credentials, significantly reducing the potential for errors and ensuring that only qualified providers are credentialed.

- **Storage and Security:** Secure storage of sensitive information is paramount in credentialing. Data management systems must comply with security standards such as HIPAA in the U.S., ensuring that personal and professional data are protected against unauthorized access or breaches.

- **Accessibility and Sharing:** While security is critical, data must also be accessible to authorized personnel when needed. Effective data management ensures that information can be easily retrieved for review, updates, or audits, facilitating collaboration among credentialing staff and other healthcare administrators.

- **Ongoing Monitoring and Updates:** Credentialing is not a one-time event but an ongoing process. Data management systems enable continuous monitoring of credential status, alerting credentialing specialists to upcoming expirations or changes in a provider's status that may require re-credentialing or further investigation.

Benefits of Effective Data Management

- **Enhanced Efficiency:** Automation and streamlined data workflows reduce manual labor, accelerate the credentialing process, and allow credentialing specialists to manage larger volumes of applications without sacrificing quality.

- **Improved Accuracy:** By minimizing manual data entry and utilizing electronic verification, the likelihood of errors is significantly reduced, enhancing the reliability of the credentialing process.

- **Regulatory Compliance:** Comprehensive data management systems help ensure that all credentialing activities are conducted in compliance with relevant laws and standards, protecting both patients and healthcare providers.

- **Strategic Decision-Making:** Access to organized and verified data supports strategic decision-making, enabling healthcare organizations to identify trends, manage risks, and allocate resources more effectively.

Implementing Data Management Solutions

When implementing data management solutions, credentialing specialists and healthcare administrators should consider the specific needs of their organization, including volume of credentialing activities, regulatory environment, and integration with existing healthcare IT infrastructure. Selecting customizable, scalable solutions with robust support and training resources can facilitate a smooth transition and ensure long-term success.

A Real-World Example

Consider a hospital system that implemented a new data management platform for its credentialing process. The platform automated the verification of licenses and certifications, securely stored provider documents, and flagged credentials due for renewal. As a result, the hospital saw a 40% reduction in credentialing processing times and a significant decrease in data discrepancies, leading to improved compliance rates and provider satisfaction.

Conclusion

Data management is indispensable to the modern medical credentialing process, offering a foundation for efficiency, accuracy, and compliance. By leveraging the right data management strategies and tools, healthcare organizations can ensure that their credentialing processes not only meet but exceed the standards required to provide safe, high-quality care to patients.

4.3. Cybersecurity Best Practices

In the digital age, cybersecurity is a paramount concern for all sectors, especially in healthcare, where the protection of sensitive information is both a legal requirement and an ethical obligation. For medical credentialing specialists, understanding and implementing cybersecurity best practices is crucial to safeguarding the integrity of the credentialing process and protecting against data breaches that could jeopardize patient safety and privacy.

Understanding the Threat Landscape

The healthcare industry is a prime target for cyberattacks due to the wealth of sensitive data it handles. Credentialing information, including personal identification, licensure, and detailed professional histories, can be exploited for identity theft, fraud, or even corporate espionage. Recognizing potential threats is the first step in defending against them.

Cybersecurity Best Practices

To mitigate the risk of cyber threats, credentialing specialists and healthcare organizations should adhere to the following best practices:

- **Regular Software Updates and Patch Management:** Ensure that all software, especially credentialing management systems and other tools used in the credentialing process, are up to date. Regular updates and patches fix vulnerabilities that could be exploited by cyber attackers.

- **Use of Strong, Unique Passwords and Multi-Factor Authentication (MFA):** Strong passwords that are regularly changed and unique to each account can significantly reduce the risk of unauthorized access. Implementing MFA adds an additional layer of security by requiring users to provide two or more verification factors to gain access to data.

- **Employee Training and Awareness Programs:** Human error remains a leading cause of data breaches. Regular training on cybersecurity awareness, phishing detection, and safe data handling practices can empower employees to be the first line of defense.

- **Data Encryption:** Encrypt sensitive data both in transit (as it moves across networks) and at rest (when stored). Encryption makes data unreadable to unauthorized individuals, protecting it even if a breach occurs.

- **Access Controls and User Authentication:** Implement strict access controls to ensure that only authorized personnel can access sensitive credentialing information. Role-based access control (RBAC) systems can limit users' access to the information necessary for their specific job functions.

- **Regular Security Audits and Vulnerability Assessments:** Conducting regular audits and assessments can help identify potential vulnerabilities in the system before they can be exploited by cyber attackers.

- **Incident Response Plan:** Have a well-defined incident response plan in place that outlines the steps to be taken in the event of a data breach. This plan should include notifying affected individuals, regulatory bodies, and taking steps to mitigate the breach's impact.

Implementing Cybersecurity Solutions

Selecting and implementing effective cybersecurity solutions requires a careful assessment of the organization's specific needs and vulnerabilities. Solutions may include advanced firewalls, intrusion detection systems, secure credentialing management platforms, and comprehensive cybersecurity insurance policies.

Real-World Application

Consider a healthcare network that experienced a phishing attack aimed at stealing credentialing information. By having cybersecurity measures in place, including employee training on phishing detection and a robust incident response plan, the network was able to quickly identify and neutralize the threat, preventing data theft and minimizing disruption to the credentialing process.

Conclusion

Cybersecurity is an integral component of modern medical credentialing, essential for protecting sensitive data from increasingly sophisticated cyber threats. By adopting best practices for cybersecurity, credentialing specialists can ensure the integrity of the credentialing process, maintain trust in the healthcare system, and contribute to the overall safety and privacy of patient care.

4.4. Exercise: 10 MCQs with Answers at the End

Multiple Choice Questions

1. What is the primary goal of implementing cybersecurity measures in medical credentialing?

   - A) To complicate the credentialing process

   - B) To protect sensitive information from cyber threats

   - C) To reduce the efficiency of the credentialing process

   - D) To increase the workload of credentialing specialists

2. Regular software updates and patch management are crucial for:

   - A) Slowing down computer systems

   - B) Fixing vulnerabilities that could be exploited by attackers

   - C) Increasing the risk of cyberattacks

   - D) Making systems incompatible with new software

3. Multi-Factor Authentication (MFA) enhances security by requiring:

  - A) The same password for all accounts

  - B) Only a simple username for access

  - C) Two or more verification factors to gain access

  - D) An easy-to-guess security question

4. The primary purpose of employee training and awareness programs in cybersecurity is to:

  - A) Increase the chance of data breaches

  - B) Reduce human error that leads to data breaches

  - C) Discourage employees from using technology

  - D) Make the credentialing process more complex

5. Data encryption is used to:

  - A) Make data easily accessible to everyone

   - B) Protect data by making it unreadable to unauthorized individuals

  - C) Increase the data processing time

  - D) Decrease data storage requirements

6. Access controls and user authentication are implemented to:

 - A) Allow all users full access to sensitive information

- B) Ensure only authorized personnel can access sensitive credentialing information

 - C) Remove any barriers to data access

 - D) Facilitate data breaches

7. Regular security audits and vulnerability assessments help to:

 - A) Identify and exploit system vulnerabilities

 - B) Ignore potential security risks

- C) Identify potential vulnerabilities before they can be exploited

 - D) Decrease system performance

8. An incident response plan is important for:

 - A) Ignoring data breaches when they occur

 - B) Quickly addressing and mitigating the impact of a data breach

 - C) Increasing the time it takes to respond to incidents

 - D) Sharing details of the breach with the public

9. The best practice for password management includes:

   - A) Using the same password across multiple systems

   - B) Choosing passwords that are easy to remember, such as "password123"

   - C) Regularly changing passwords and using strong, unique passwords for each account

   - D) Writing down passwords and storing them in visible locations

10. Why are regular training and awareness programs for staff critical in cybersecurity?

   - A) They ensure that staff are the weakest link in the security chain

   - B) They keep staff informed about the latest cyber threats and safe data handling practices

   - C) They are not necessary but recommended for compliance reasons

   - D) They provide a formal setting for staff to socialize

Answers

1. B) To protect sensitive information from cyber threats

2. B) Fixing vulnerabilities that could be exploited by attackers

3. C) Two or more verification factors to gain access

4. B) Reduce human error that leads to data breaches

5. B) Protect data by making it unreadable to unauthorized individuals

6. B) Ensure only authorized personnel can access sensitive credentialing information

7. C) Identify potential vulnerabilities before they can be exploited

8. B) Quickly addressing and mitigating the impact of a data breach

9. C) Regularly changing passwords and using strong, unique passwords for each account

10. B) They keep staff informed about the latest cyber threats and safe data handling practices

These questions highlight the importance of cybersecurity in the medical credentialing process, emphasizing the need for ongoing vigilance, regular updates, and comprehensive training to protect sensitive information against cyber threats.

Chapter 5: Credentialing in Different Healthcare Settings

5.1. Hospitals and Acute Care Centers

The Distinctive Environment of Hospitals and Acute Care Centers

Credentialing in hospitals and acute care centers is a critical component of healthcare management, ensuring that all medical professionals are qualified to provide high-quality care in these fast-paced and high-stakes environments. These settings require healthcare providers to have specific qualifications, skills, and experience to handle the acute health needs of patients, including emergencies, surgeries, and other complex medical conditions.

Key Aspects of Credentialing in These Settings

- **Rigorous Credentialing Standards:** Hospitals and acute care centers often have more stringent credentialing standards due to the complex nature of care they provide. This includes thorough verification of educational backgrounds, licensure, board certifications, and specialized training. The goal is to ensure that healthcare providers are equipped to make critical decisions and perform high-risk procedures with expertise and confidence.

- **Privileging Process:** Beyond basic credentialing, these settings also implement a privileging process, which is the authorization for healthcare providers to perform specific procedures or services based on their credentials, training, and competence. Privileges are carefully assessed and granted according to the provider's experience and the facility's needs, ensuring patient safety and quality of care.

- **Continuous Monitoring:** Given the dynamic nature of hospital and acute care settings, continuous monitoring of healthcare providers' credentials and performance is essential. This includes regular reviews of licensure status, compliance with continuing education requirements, and evaluations of clinical performance and patient outcomes.

- **Emergency Credentialing:** In situations where immediate care is necessary, such as a natural disaster or pandemic, hospitals and acute care centers may implement emergency credentialing procedures. These expedited processes allow for the rapid onboarding of healthcare providers to meet increased demand, while still ensuring that they meet essential qualifications and standards.

- **Collaboration with Medical Staff:** Credentialing in these environments involves close collaboration with medical staff leadership, such as chief medical officers and department heads, to assess the competencies and needs of the clinical team. This collaboration ensures that credentialing processes align with clinical goals and patient care standards.

Challenges and Solutions

Credentialing in hospitals and acute care centers faces unique challenges, including managing a large and diverse pool of healthcare providers, adapting to rapid technological and medical advancements, and ensuring compliance with stringent regulatory standards. Addressing these challenges requires a robust credentialing system, efficient processes, and ongoing communication and collaboration among administrative and medical staff.

Implementing Best Practices

- **Utilizing Technology:** Leveraging advanced credentialing software and tools can streamline the credentialing and privileging processes, enhance accuracy, and improve efficiency.

- **Standardizing Processes:** Developing and adhering to standardized credentialing and privileging procedures ensures consistency, fairness, and compliance with healthcare regulations and standards.

- **Fostering Team Collaboration:** Encouraging active collaboration and communication between credentialing staff and medical leadership facilitates a comprehensive understanding of clinical needs and enhances the credentialing process's effectiveness.

Conclusion

Credentialing in hospitals and acute care centers is a complex but essential process that directly impacts patient safety and the quality of healthcare services. By adhering to rigorous standards, implementing efficient processes, and utilizing technology, these healthcare settings can ensure that their medical staff are well-qualified to meet the acute and diverse needs of their patient populations.

5.2. Outpatient Clinics and Ambulatory Care

Adapting Credentialing to Outpatient and Ambulatory Settings

Credentialing in outpatient clinics and ambulatory care centers plays a pivotal role in ensuring the delivery of safe, efficient, and high-quality care in settings outside traditional hospital environments. These healthcare facilities, which include walk-in clinics, specialized outpatient centers, and ambulatory surgery centers, cater to patients requiring medical services without the need for overnight hospitalization. The credentialing process in these settings must be tailored to meet the specific needs of a more diverse patient population and a wide range of medical services.

Key Considerations for Credentialing

- **Scope of Services:** Credentialing processes must align with the broad scope of services offered, from routine health examinations to specialized procedures. This requires verifying that healthcare providers have the appropriate qualifications, certifications, and experience for the specific services they will provide.

- **Quality and Safety Standards:** While outpatient and ambulatory care centers may not handle complex surgical procedures requiring extended hospital stays, the emphasis on quality and patient safety is equally stringent. Credentialing ensures adherence to these standards by verifying providers' competencies and compliance with clinical guidelines.

- **Efficient Process Management:** Given the typically high volume of patients and the wide variety of services offered, these settings demand a more streamlined and efficient credentialing process. This efficiency ensures that qualified providers are available to meet patient needs promptly, without compromising the thoroughness of the credentialing process.

- **Regulatory Compliance:** Outpatient clinics and ambulatory care centers are subject to specific regulatory requirements and accreditation standards. Credentialing processes must ensure that all providers meet these requirements, which may vary depending on the state and the type of services offered.

Challenges and Strategies

Credentialing for outpatient and ambulatory care settings faces unique challenges, including managing provider credentials across a variety of specialties and ensuring rapid yet thorough credential verification to meet patient demand. Strategies to address these challenges include:

- **Leveraging Technology:** Utilizing credentialing software that can automate and streamline the verification process, manage documents, and track credential expiration dates is critical for efficiency and accuracy.

- **Customized Privileging:** Developing a privileging system tailored to the specific services offered, ensuring providers are authorized to perform only those procedures for which they are qualified.

- **Regular Updates and Training:** Keeping abreast of changes in regulatory standards and ensuring that all staff are regularly trained on these updates and on the importance of compliance in the credentialing process.

Best Practices for Success

- **Collaboration with Professional Organizations:** Working closely with professional organizations and specialty boards can help ensure that credentialing standards are up-to-date and reflective of best practices in each specialty.

- **Continuous Quality Improvement:** Implementing a continuous quality improvement (CQI) approach to credentialing can help identify areas for process enhancement, improving efficiency and reducing the risk of errors.

- **Patient-Centered Focus:** Keeping the patient experience at the forefront of credentialing efforts ensures that processes not only comply with regulatory standards but also contribute to the overall quality of care and patient satisfaction.

Conclusion

The credentialing process in outpatient clinics and ambulatory care settings is essential for maintaining high standards of care, ensuring patient safety, and complying with regulatory requirements. By adapting credentialing practices to the unique needs of these settings, healthcare organizations can provide a wide range of quality services efficiently and effectively. Through the use of technology, customized privileging, and continuous improvement, credentialing can support the dynamic environment of outpatient and ambulatory care, ensuring that patients receive the best possible care from qualified professionals.

5.3. Telehealth and Remote Care Providers

Evolving Credentialing for Digital Health Services

The rise of telehealth and remote care services has transformed healthcare delivery, making medical advice and treatment more accessible and convenient for patients. This digital shift necessitates an evolution in credentialing processes to address the unique challenges and opportunities presented by telehealth. Credentialing for telehealth and remote care providers ensures that practitioners who deliver care through digital platforms meet the same high standards of quality and professionalism as those in traditional settings.

Key Credentialing Considerations in Telehealth

- **Licensure Across Jurisdictions:** Telehealth providers often serve patients in multiple states, requiring a careful understanding of state-specific licensure requirements. Credentialing processes must verify that providers are licensed to practice in the patient's location, adhering to the legal and regulatory frameworks governing telehealth services.

- **Technology Competency:** Beyond clinical skills, telehealth credentialing must assess providers' competency with digital communication tools and platforms. This includes their ability to use telehealth software effectively, maintain patient privacy, and adhere to cybersecurity best practices.

- **Quality and Continuity of Care:** Credentialing for telehealth must ensure that providers can deliver the same level of care quality as in-person services. This involves evaluating their ability to establish patient-provider relationships, assess patient conditions accurately, and follow up on care plans remotely.

- **Interdisciplinary Collaboration:** Telehealth services often involve coordination between multiple healthcare professionals and specialties. Credentialing processes should consider providers' ability to collaborate effectively in a virtual healthcare team, ensuring comprehensive patient care.

Addressing Challenges in Telehealth Credentialing

Telehealth credentialing faces specific challenges, including navigating diverse regulatory environments and ensuring providers are adept at delivering care virtually. Strategies to address these challenges include:

- **Utilizing Centralized Credentialing Databases:** Centralized databases can streamline the verification of licensure and certifications across states, making it easier to credential providers for telehealth services.

- **Adapting Training and Assessment:** Credentialing programs may need to incorporate training and assessment modules focused on telehealth competencies, including digital literacy, remote patient engagement, and virtual ethics.

- **Enhancing Interoperability:** Ensuring that credentialing information is interoperable across healthcare systems and telehealth platforms can facilitate smoother credentialing processes and provider integration.

Best Practices for Telehealth Credentialing

- **Comprehensive Policy Development:** Establishing clear policies and guidelines for telehealth credentialing can help standardize processes, ensuring consistency and compliance across jurisdictions.

- **Regular Policy and Process Review:** Given the rapidly evolving nature of telehealth, regular reviews of credentialing policies and processes are essential to adapt to new technologies, regulatory changes, and best practices.

- **Emphasizing Privacy and Security:** Credentialing for telehealth must prioritize providers' understanding and commitment to patient privacy and data security, reflecting the heightened importance of cybersecurity in digital health services.

Conclusion

Credentialing for telehealth and remote care providers is a critical component of ensuring safe, effective, and high-quality digital health services. As telehealth continues to grow, credentialing processes must evolve to address the unique aspects of virtual care delivery. By focusing on licensure, technology competency, and quality of care, healthcare organizations can foster trust in telehealth services, ensuring patients receive the best possible care, regardless of location.

5.4. Exercise: 10 MCQs with Answers at the End

Multiple Choice Questions

1. What is the primary goal of credentialing in healthcare?

  - A) To increase administrative tasks

  - B) To ensure healthcare providers meet required standards

  - C) To limit the number of healthcare providers

  - D) To complicate the healthcare delivery system

2. Credentialing in hospitals and acute care centers often requires:

   - A) Less stringent standards than other healthcare settings

   - B) Only a basic background check

   - C) Verification of specialized training and competencies

   - D) Ignoring previous disciplinary actions

3. In outpatient clinics, credentialing focuses on:

   - A) Reducing the quality of care for efficiency

   - B) Providers' ability to perform a wide range of services

   - C) Only the administrative aspects of care

   - D) Decreasing patient satisfaction

4. Telehealth credentialing uniquely requires assessing a provider's:

   - A) Preference for traditional care methods

   - B) Competency with digital communication tools

   - C) Ability to avoid using technology

   - D) Interest in relocating to different states

5. Which is a challenge unique to credentialing for telehealth services?

   - A) Ignoring state-specific licensure requirements

   - B) Navigating diverse regulatory environments

   - C) Focusing solely on in-person care standards

   - D) Limiting access to digital health platforms

6. Continuous monitoring in credentialing is essential for:

   - A) Creating more work for credentialing specialists

   - B) Ensuring ongoing compliance and quality of care

   - C) Discouraging healthcare providers from maintaining their credentials

   - D) Reducing the importance of initial credentialing

7. Emergency credentialing procedures are implemented in response to:

   - A) The preference of healthcare providers

   - B) A surplus of healthcare workers

   - C) Immediate care needs during crises

   - D) Administrative convenience

8. Effective telehealth credentialing should ensure providers can:

   - A) Only communicate via email

   - B) Establish patient-provider relationships remotely

   - C) Avoid using secure platforms for patient interactions

   - D) Provide care without licensure

9. Centralized credentialing databases facilitate:

   - A) Slower verification processes

   - B) Verification of licensure and certifications across states

   - C) Increased risk of data breaches

   - D) Less accurate credentialing information

10. A primary focus of credentialing in all healthcare settings is:

   - A) Maximizing administrative costs

   - B) Reducing the standards of care

   - C) Ensuring patient safety and quality of care

   - D) Discouraging the use of technology in healthcare

Answers

1. B) To ensure healthcare providers meet required standards

2. C) Verification of specialized training and competencies

3. B) Providers' ability to perform a wide range of services

4. B) Competency with digital communication tools

5. B) Navigating diverse regulatory environments

6. B) Ensuring ongoing compliance and quality of care

7. C) Immediate care needs during crises

8. B) Establish patient-provider relationships remotely

9. B) Verification of licensure and certifications across states

10. C) Ensuring patient safety and quality of care

These questions are designed to test your understanding of the complexities and priorities of credentialing across different healthcare settings, emphasizing the universal goal of maintaining high standards of care and patient safety.

Chapter 6: Working with Insurance Companies

6.1. Understanding Insurance Requirements

The Intersection of Credentialing and Insurance

Credentialing plays a crucial role not only in verifying the qualifications of healthcare providers but also in facilitating their participation in insurance networks. Understanding insurance requirements is essential for credentialing specialists, as these criteria often dictate which providers can offer services to a broader patient base through insurance coverage. This integration between credentialing and insurance underscores the importance of navigating insurance standards and processes effectively.

Key Insurance Requirements for Providers

- **Accreditation and Licensure:** Insurance companies typically require that healthcare providers be fully licensed in their state and, where applicable, accredited by relevant bodies. This ensures that providers meet the minimum standards for delivering care.

- **Board Certification:** Many insurers prefer or require that providers be board certified in their specialty. This certification serves as an additional layer of assurance regarding the provider's expertise and commitment to ongoing education.

- **Quality Metrics:** Insurance companies may assess providers based on specific quality metrics, such as patient satisfaction scores, treatment outcomes, and adherence to evidence-based practices. These metrics help insurers identify providers who deliver high-quality, cost-effective care.

- **Malpractice Insurance:** Carrying adequate malpractice insurance is often a prerequisite for joining an insurance network. This protects both the provider and the insurer in the event of a legal claim.

- **Data Security Compliance:** With the increasing emphasis on digital health records, insurers require providers to comply with data security standards, such as the Health Insurance Portability and Accountability Act (HIPAA) in the United States.

Navigating the Credentialing Process with Insurers

The process of credentialing with insurance companies involves several steps, including:

- **Application Submission:** Providers must submit detailed applications to each insurer, including documentation of their qualifications, licensure, and other relevant information.

- **Verification and Review:** Insurance companies conduct their verification process, similar to hospital or clinic credentialing, reviewing the provider's credentials, background, and performance metrics.

- **Contract Negotiation:** Once approved, providers often enter into a contract negotiation phase, where terms of reimbursement rates, network participation, and other details are finalized.

- **Continuous Compliance:** Providers must maintain compliance with insurance requirements, including ongoing quality metrics and re-credentialing processes, to remain in the network.

Challenges and Solutions

One of the primary challenges in working with insurance companies is the diversity of requirements and processes across different insurers. Credentialing specialists can address this challenge by:

- **Maintaining Updated Provider Information:** Keeping provider credentials and documentation up to date simplifies the application and re-credentialing processes.

- **Leveraging Technology:** Credentialing management systems can streamline the submission and tracking of applications across multiple insurers.

- **Understanding Each Insurer's Criteria:** Developing a comprehensive understanding of each insurer's specific requirements can help credentialing specialists prepare applications more effectively and anticipate potential issues.

Conclusion

Understanding and meeting insurance requirements is a critical aspect of the credentialing process, impacting providers' ability to serve insured patients and participate in healthcare networks. By navigating these requirements effectively, credentialing specialists play a vital role in ensuring that healthcare providers can offer accessible, high-quality care to a wider patient population.

6.2. The Role of Credentialing in Billing and Reimbursement

Integrating Credentialing with Financial Operations

The process of credentialing is not only a cornerstone for ensuring quality and compliance in healthcare delivery but also plays a pivotal role in the financial operations of healthcare practices, particularly in billing and reimbursement. Proper credentialing directly impacts a healthcare provider's ability to bill insurance companies for services rendered and receive reimbursement, making it a critical element in the sustainability and success of healthcare operations.

Credentialing and Its Impact on Reimbursement

- **Eligibility for Insurance Networks:** Providers must be credentialed with insurance companies to become part of their networks. Being in-network allows providers to bill for services covered under patients' insurance plans, ensuring a steady flow of reimbursements.

- **Reimbursement Rates:** Credentialing can also influence the negotiation of reimbursement rates with insurance companies. Credentialed providers in good standing may have the leverage to negotiate more favorable terms, directly impacting their revenue.

- **Compliance with Payer Requirements:** Each insurer has specific credentialing criteria that providers must meet to bill for their services. Failure to comply with these requirements can result in denied claims, delayed payments, and increased administrative costs.

The Credentialing Process and Billing

- **Verification of Credentials:** Insurance companies verify the credentials of healthcare providers to ensure they meet the necessary qualifications and standards. This verification is a prerequisite for billing insurance for patient care services.

- **Contractual Agreements:** Once credentialed, providers often enter into contractual agreements with insurers, outlining the terms of reimbursement, billing procedures, and the scope of covered services.

- **Provider Enrollment:** Credentialing is followed by provider enrollment, the process of officially registering with an insurance company as an approved provider. This step is crucial for being listed as an in-network provider and for initiating the billing process.

Challenges in Credentialing for Billing

- **Complexity of Insurance Requirements:** The diversity of requirements across different insurance companies can complicate the credentialing process, leading to potential delays in becoming an approved provider.

- **Maintaining Up-to-Date Credentials:** Continuous maintenance of up-to-date credentials is necessary to avoid disruptions in billing and reimbursement. This requires diligent monitoring and timely renewal of licenses, certifications, and insurance contracts.

- **Coordination Between Credentialing and Billing Departments:** Effective communication and coordination between credentialing and billing departments are vital to ensure that all provider credentials are current and accurately reflected in billing systems.

Strategies for Optimizing Credentialing and Billing

- **Leveraging Technology:** Utilizing advanced credentialing and billing software can streamline processes, reduce errors, and expedite reimbursements.

- **Regular Training and Education:** Keeping credentialing and billing staff informed about changes in insurance regulations, billing practices, and credentialing requirements can help minimize disruptions.

- **Proactive Credentialing Management:** Implementing proactive strategies for managing credential renewals, insurance company notifications, and contract negotiations can prevent lapses in billing eligibility.

Conclusion

The role of credentialing in billing and reimbursement is a critical aspect of healthcare administration, directly affecting a provider's revenue stream and financial health. By understanding and effectively managing the intricacies of the credentialing process, healthcare providers can ensure seamless billing operations, optimize reimbursement rates, and maintain a stable financial foundation in the competitive healthcare market.

6.3. Navigating Insurance Networks

Understanding the Complex Landscape

Navigating insurance networks is a critical task for healthcare providers and credentialing specialists. These networks, established by insurance companies, consist of healthcare providers that have been credentialed and contracted to provide services to insured individuals. Being part of an insurance network not only broadens a provider's patient base but also impacts reimbursement rates and billing practices. Understanding how to effectively navigate these networks is essential for maximizing healthcare delivery and financial performance.

Key Strategies for Effective Navigation

- **Thoroughly Understand Network Requirements:** Each insurance network has its own set of requirements and standards for joining. Providers should understand these criteria thoroughly, including necessary qualifications, documentation, and the application process, to increase their chances of acceptance.

- **Stay Informed About Changes:** Insurance networks frequently update their policies, reimbursement rates, and contract terms. Staying informed about these changes is crucial for maintaining good standing in the network and ensuring accurate billing and reimbursement.

- **Build Strong Relationships with Insurers:** Establishing and maintaining positive relationships with insurance companies can facilitate smoother negotiations, quicker resolution of issues, and potentially better contract terms. Regular communication and prompt response to insurers' requests can strengthen these relationships.

- **Leverage Credentialing Specialists:** Credentialing specialists play a vital role in navigating insurance networks. Their expertise in the credentialing process, understanding of insurance requirements, and ability to manage paperwork and deadlines can significantly ease the burden on healthcare providers.

- **Optimize Provider Enrollment:** Beyond initial credentialing, provider enrollment is the process of officially registering with an insurance company as an approved provider. Ensuring that this process is handled efficiently and accurately is essential for starting and continuing a successful relationship with an insurance network.

- **Understand the Appeals Process:** Familiarity with the appeals process for denied claims or disputes over reimbursement rates is important. Knowing how to present information effectively and who to contact can make the appeals process more manageable and increase the likelihood of a favorable outcome.

Challenges and Solutions

Navigating insurance networks comes with its challenges, including complex application processes, frequent policy changes, and sometimes lengthy negotiations over contract terms. Solutions to these challenges include:

- **Utilizing Technology:** Implementing advanced software solutions for credentialing and billing can streamline processes, reduce errors, and improve efficiency in managing insurance network requirements.

- **Continuing Education:** Engaging in continuous education and training on healthcare insurance policies, billing practices, and regulatory changes can help providers and credentialing specialists stay ahead of the curve.

- **Collaborative Efforts:** Working collaboratively within healthcare organizations, including finance, legal, and clinical teams, can provide a multidisciplinary approach to navigating insurance networks effectively.

Conclusion

Successfully navigating insurance networks is essential for healthcare providers to access a wider patient base, ensure financial stability, and deliver high-quality care. By understanding network requirements, maintaining strong insurer relationships, and leveraging the expertise of credentialing specialists, healthcare providers can effectively manage their participation in insurance networks. Overcoming the challenges of this complex landscape requires ongoing effort, adaptability, and strategic planning, but the rewards in terms of patient access and financial performance are substantial.

6.4. Exercise: 10 MCQs with Answers at the End

Multiple Choice Questions

1. What is the primary purpose of healthcare providers joining insurance networks?

   - A) To limit the number of patients they see

   - B) To increase administrative paperwork

   - C) To expand their patient base and ensure reimbursement

   - D) To decrease their service offerings

2. Which of the following is NOT a requirement for joining an insurance network?

   - A) Having a valid medical license

   - B) Paying a membership fee to patients

   - C) Being board certified in a specialty (if applicable)

   - D) Carrying adequate malpractice insurance

3. What role do credentialing specialists play in navigating insurance networks?

   - A) They increase the complexity of the process

   - B) They manage the paperwork and ensure compliance with network requirements

   - C) They discourage providers from joining networks

   - D) They solely focus on legal disputes

4. Why is it important for healthcare providers to stay informed about changes in insurance policies?

- A) To ensure they are billing correctly and maximizing reimbursement

   - B) Changes in policies do not affect healthcare providers

   - C) To reduce the quality of care provided

   - D) To avoid building relationships with insurance companies

5. What is the provider enrollment process associated with?

   - A) Ending a contract with an insurance network

   - B) Officially registering with an insurance company as an approved provider

   - C) Decreasing the provider's patient base

   - D) Simplifying legal disputes with insurance companies

6. Building strong relationships with insurers can lead to:

- A) Slower claim processing times

- B) Reduced access to patients

- C) More favorable contract terms and quicker issue resolution

- D) Increased administrative errors

7. Familiarity with the appeals process is important for:

- A) Only new healthcare providers

- B) Ignoring denied claims

- C) Effectively disputing denied claims or reimbursement disputes

- D) Decreasing the quality of patient care

8. Utilizing technology in managing insurance network requirements can help:

- A) Increase errors in billing and credentialing

- B) Streamline processes and improve efficiency

- C) Discourage providers from updating their credentials

- D) Complicate the provider enrollment process

9. Continuous education on healthcare insurance policies and billing practices is vital for:

   - A) Only administrative staff

   - B) Reducing the provider's credibility

   - C) Staying ahead of regulatory and policy changes

   - D) Ignoring updates in the healthcare industry

10. A multidisciplinary approach to navigating insurance networks often includes collaboration between:

   - A) Finance, legal, and clinical teams

   - B) Only external consultants

   - C) Competing healthcare providers

   - D) Patients and non-medical staff

Answers

1. C) To expand their patient base and ensure reimbursement

2. B) Paying a membership fee to patients

3. B) They manage the paperwork and ensure compliance with network requirements

4. A) To ensure they are billing correctly and maximizing reimbursement

5. B) Officially registering with an insurance company as an approved provider

6. C) More favorable contract terms and quicker issue resolution

7. C) Effectively disputing denied claims or reimbursement disputes

8. B) Streamline processes and improve efficiency

9. C) Staying ahead of regulatory and policy changes

10. A) Finance, legal, and clinical teams

These questions and answers highlight the critical aspects of working with insurance companies and navigating insurance networks, underscoring the importance of understanding insurance requirements, building strong relationships with insurers, and leveraging technology and education to improve efficiency and outcomes.

Chapter 7: Continuing Education and Certification

7.1. Importance of Ongoing Professional Development

The Lifeline of Healthcare Expertise

Ongoing professional development and certification are indispensable in the ever-evolving field of healthcare. For medical credentialing specialists and healthcare providers alike, continuous education is not just a requirement but a commitment to excellence, patient safety, and the advancement of healthcare standards. This commitment ensures that professionals remain at the forefront of medical knowledge, technological advancements, and best practices in patient care.

Enhancing Competence and Confidence

- **Staying Updated with Medical Advances:** The healthcare industry is characterized by rapid advancements in medical research, treatment methodologies, and technology. Ongoing professional development ensures that healthcare providers keep pace with these changes, enhancing their competence in delivering state-of-the-art care.

- **Fulfilling Licensure and Certification Requirements:** Many healthcare professions require continuous education as part of licensure and certification renewal processes. These requirements, set by professional boards and regulatory agencies, aim to maintain high standards of professional practice.

- **Improving Patient Outcomes:** There is a direct correlation between continuous professional development and improved patient outcomes. Education and training in the latest clinical practices and technologies enable healthcare providers to offer more effective, efficient, and safe patient care.

- **Professional Growth and Career Advancement:** Engaging in ongoing education and achieving advanced certifications open pathways for professional growth. They provide opportunities for career advancement, leadership roles, and specialization in niche areas of healthcare.

Strategies for Effective Professional Development

- **Identifying Learning Needs:** Healthcare professionals should regularly assess their knowledge and skills to identify areas where further education and training are needed. This could be driven by changes in their practice area, new healthcare regulations, or personal career goals.

- **Leveraging Multiple Learning Formats:** Professional development can be pursued through various formats, including online courses, workshops, seminars, conferences, and peer review activities. Diversifying learning formats can enhance engagement and accommodate different learning styles.

- **Integrating Learning into Practice:** Applying new knowledge and skills in clinical practice is crucial. Simulation training, peer mentoring, and reflective practice are effective ways to integrate learning and improve clinical competence.

- **Maintaining Certification:** Credentialing specialists and healthcare providers should stay informed about the requirements for maintaining their professional certifications. This often involves completing a certain number of continuing education units (CEUs) or participating in specific training programs.

Challenges and Solutions

- **Finding Time for Education:** Balancing professional responsibilities with ongoing learning can be challenging. Solutions include prioritizing learning activities, time management strategies, and seeking employer support for education initiatives.

- **Ensuring Quality of Education:** With the proliferation of continuing education options, ensuring the quality and relevance of educational programs is vital. Healthcare professionals should seek programs accredited by recognized bodies in their field.

- **Measuring Impact:** Assessing the impact of professional development on clinical practice and patient care can be complex. Regular feedback, performance evaluations, and patient outcomes data can help measure the effectiveness of educational endeavors.

Conclusion

Ongoing professional development and certification are fundamental to maintaining the competence and professionalism of healthcare providers and credentialing specialists. By committing to continuous learning, individuals not only enhance their own careers but also contribute to the overall quality and safety of healthcare delivery. Embracing a culture of lifelong learning is essential for navigating the complexities of modern healthcare and fulfilling the commitment to patient care excellence.

7.2. Certification Programs for Credentialing Specialists

Elevating Professional Standards and Expertise

Certification programs for credentialing specialists are designed to formalize the expertise required to navigate the complex credentialing processes in healthcare. These programs not only affirm a specialist's knowledge and skills but also elevate the professional standards of the credentialing field. By obtaining certification, credentialing specialists demonstrate their commitment to excellence, adherence to industry best practices, and dedication to ensuring the competence and quality of healthcare providers.

Key Certification Programs

- **Certified Provider Credentialing Specialist (CPCS):** Offered by the National Association Medical Staff Services (NAMSS), the CPCS certification is a recognized standard for individuals involved in the credentialing of medical staff and allied health professionals. It validates the specialist's expertise in credentialing processes, privileging, medical staff organization, and compliance with accreditation and regulatory requirements.

- **Certified Professional Medical Services Management (CPMSM):** Also provided by NAMSS, the CPMSM certification is aimed at professionals who manage medical services or medical staff services departments. This certification focuses on leadership skills, governance, legal and regulatory compliance, and the management of credentialing services.

Benefits of Certification

- **Recognition of Professional Competence:** Certification acknowledges a credentialing specialist's proficiency and commitment to maintaining the highest standards of practice in the credentialing field.

- **Career Advancement:** Certified specialists often have a competitive edge in the job market, with enhanced prospects for career advancement, leadership roles, and increased compensation.

- **Improved Healthcare Quality and Safety:** Certification programs equip specialists with the knowledge and skills necessary to ensure that healthcare providers meet all required qualifications, thereby contributing to improved patient care quality and safety.

- **Professional Development:** Preparing for and maintaining certification encourages ongoing professional development and continuous learning, keeping specialists abreast of the latest trends, regulations, and best practices in healthcare credentialing.

Preparing for Certification

- **Eligibility Requirements:** Candidates must typically meet specific educational and professional experience criteria to be eligible for certification exams. These requirements can vary by program, so it's important to review them carefully.

- **Study and Preparation:** Many organizations offer study guides, courses, and workshops to help candidates prepare for the certification exams. Engaging with these resources can significantly increase the likelihood of success.

- **Continuing Education:** To maintain certification, specialists are usually required to complete a certain number of continuing education units (CEUs) within a specified period. This requirement encourages professionals to engage in lifelong learning and stay updated on industry changes.

Challenges and Opportunities

While pursuing certification can be challenging due to the need for study time and the cost of exam fees, the benefits significantly outweigh these obstacles. Certification opens doors to professional growth, enhances credibility in the field, and contributes to the overall improvement of healthcare quality and patient safety.

Conclusion

Certification programs for credentialing specialists play a crucial role in standardizing the knowledge and skills necessary for effective healthcare credentialing. By achieving certification, specialists not only enhance their own professional development but also contribute to the integrity and quality of healthcare delivery. As the healthcare landscape continues to evolve, the demand for certified credentialing specialists is likely to grow, highlighting the importance of these programs in promoting excellence in healthcare credentialing.

7.3. Staying Current with Healthcare Trends

The Imperative of Continuous Learning

In the dynamic field of healthcare, staying informed about current trends, technological advancements, regulatory changes, and best practices is crucial for professionals. For credentialing specialists, understanding these trends is not just about maintaining relevance; it's about ensuring the quality and safety of healthcare delivery. The ability to anticipate and adapt to changes in the healthcare landscape can significantly impact the credentialing process and the overall effectiveness of healthcare services.

Key Strategies for Staying Informed

- **Professional Associations and Journals:** Membership in professional associations such as the National Association Medical Staff Services (NAMSS) provides access to a wealth of resources, including journals, newsletters, and research publications that cover the latest developments in healthcare credentialing and management.

- **Continuing Education:** Participating in webinars, workshops, conferences, and online courses is an excellent way to stay abreast of new trends and earn continuing education units (CEUs) required for maintaining certification.

- **Networking:** Engaging with peers through professional networking events, online forums, and social media groups can provide valuable insights into emerging trends and challenges in healthcare credentialing.

- **Regulatory Updates:** Keeping track of changes in healthcare regulations and accreditation standards is essential. Government and regulatory agency websites, as well as industry news outlets, are reliable sources for updates.

- **Technology Advancements:** With digital health technologies evolving rapidly, credentialing specialists must understand how these tools can impact credentialing processes and healthcare delivery. Following tech news in healthcare can provide early insights into beneficial technologies.

Impact of Staying Current

- **Enhanced Credentialing Processes:** Understanding the latest trends in healthcare allows credentialing specialists to streamline processes, improve efficiency, and ensure that credentialing standards align with current best practices.

- **Improved Compliance:** Staying informed about regulatory changes ensures that healthcare organizations remain compliant, reducing the risk of penalties and enhancing patient safety.

- **Better Decision Making:** Knowledge of the latest developments in healthcare can inform better decision-making, particularly when integrating new technologies or adapting to changes in healthcare delivery models.

- **Professional Growth:** Continuous learning contributes to professional development, opening up opportunities for career advancement and leadership roles within the healthcare credentialing field.

Challenges and Solutions

While the importance of staying current is clear, healthcare professionals face challenges such as time constraints and information overload. Solutions include:

- **Prioritizing Learning:** Allocating specific times for learning and professional development can help manage time effectively. Employers can support this by providing learning opportunities and resources.

- **Selective Focus:** Given the vast amount of information available, focusing on high-quality, relevant sources can help reduce information overload. Curating a list of trusted publications and websites can streamline the process of staying informed.

- **Leveraging Technology:** Utilizing apps and platforms that aggregate and personalize industry news can make it easier to keep up with relevant trends without overwhelming daily workflows.

Conclusion

Staying current with healthcare trends is a continuous commitment for credentialing specialists and healthcare professionals. It requires a proactive approach to learning and adaptation, leveraging resources and networks to keep abreast of the changes shaping healthcare. By embracing continuous learning, professionals can contribute to the advancement of healthcare quality, compliance, and efficiency, ensuring they remain valuable assets to their organizations and the patients they serve.

7.4. Exercise: 10 MCQs with Answers at the End

Creating a set of 10 multiple-choice questions (MCQs) with answers at the end provides an effective way to review and reinforce the key concepts discussed in the chapter on "Continuing Education and Certification," particularly focusing on the importance of ongoing professional development. Here are the MCQs designed to test comprehension and retention of the material covered:

Multiple Choice Questions

1. What is the primary purpose of ongoing professional development for healthcare professionals?

   - A) To increase their salary

   - B) To meet new people

   - C) To stay updated with healthcare trends and advancements

   - D) To reduce their workload

2. Which organization offers the Certified Provider Credentialing Specialist (CPCS) certification?

   - A) American Medical Association (AMA)

   - B) National Association Medical Staff Services (NAMSS)

   - C) World Health Organization (WHO)

   - D) American Nurses Credentialing Center (ANCC)

3. Continuous education in healthcare helps professionals:

   - A) Avoid patient contact

   - B) Improve patient outcomes

   - C) Work fewer hours

   - D) Ignore healthcare regulations

4. Membership in professional associations benefits credentialing specialists by:

   - A) Limiting their access to information

   - B) Providing resources like journals and research publications

   - C) Decreasing their credibility

   - D) Isolating them from industry trends

5. Which strategy is NOT effective for staying current with healthcare trends?

   - A) Networking with peers

   - B) Ignoring regulatory updates

   - C) Attending webinars and conferences

   - D) Reading professional journals

6. The impact of not staying informed about regulatory changes in healthcare could result in:

   - A) More vacation time

   - B) Reduced risk of penalties

   - C) Enhanced patient safety

   - D) Non-compliance and potential penalties

7. One of the challenges in maintaining ongoing professional development is:

 - A) Too few resources available

 - B) Time constraints and information overload

 - C) Lack of available certifications

 - D) Mandatory retirement policies

8. Technology advancements in healthcare:

 - A) Are irrelevant to credentialing specialists

 - B) Can simplify credentialing processes

 - C) Decrease the quality of care

 - D) Are only important for IT professionals

9. An effective way to manage information overload is to:

 - A) Stop reading industry news

 - B) Focus on high-quality, relevant sources

 - C) Ignore updates from professional associations

 - D) Only listen to word of mouth

10. Continuous learning and professional development:

 - A) Have no impact on career advancement

 - B) Are only required at the start of a healthcare career

- C) Contribute to professional growth and opportunities for advancement

- D) Discourage innovation in healthcare practices

Answers

1. C) To stay updated with healthcare trends and advancements

2. B) National Association Medical Staff Services (NAMSS)

3. B) Improve patient outcomes

4. B) Providing resources like journals and research publications

5. B) Ignoring regulatory updates

6. D) Non-compliance and potential penalties

7. B) Time constraints and information overload

8. B) Can simplify credentialing processes

9. B) Focus on high-quality, relevant sources

10. C) Contribute to professional growth and opportunities for advancement

These questions are designed to reinforce the key points about the critical role of ongoing professional development, certification, and the strategies for staying current in the rapidly evolving field of healthcare.

Chapter 8: Communication and Interpersonal Skills

8.1. Effective Communication with Healthcare Professionals

The Cornerstone of Successful Credentialing

Effective communication is vital in the healthcare environment, particularly in the credentialing process, where clear, concise, and accurate exchanges between credentialing specialists and healthcare professionals are crucial. This communication ensures that credentialing processes are completed efficiently and accurately, supporting the delivery of high-quality patient care.

Key Elements of Effective Communication

- **Clarity and Conciseness:** Messages should be clear and to the point to avoid misunderstandings. Credentialing involves complex information that needs to be understood by all parties involved.

- **Active Listening:** This involves fully concentrating, understanding, responding, and then remembering what is being said. Active listening in credentialing can prevent errors and oversights in the documentation and application process.

- **Professional Tone:** Maintaining a professional tone, even in written communications, fosters respect and facilitates smoother interactions. This is especially important when addressing sensitive issues or discrepancies in documentation.

- **Timely Responses:** Prompt responses to inquiries and submissions are essential for keeping the credentialing process on track and for building trust with healthcare professionals.

- **Empathy and Understanding:** Recognizing the pressures and challenges faced by healthcare professionals, especially in providing patient care, can help credentialing specialists approach communications with empathy and understanding.

Strategies for Improving Communication

- **Regular Training:** Providing credentialing specialists and healthcare professionals with regular training on communication skills can enhance the effectiveness of interactions.

- **Use of Technology:** Leveraging technology, such as secure messaging platforms and email, can streamline communications, making it easier to share documents and provide updates on the credentialing process.

- **Feedback Mechanisms:** Implementing mechanisms for feedback on the communication process can identify areas for improvement and help tailor approaches to better meet the needs of healthcare professionals.

- **Documentation:** Keeping detailed records of all communications related to credentialing ensures that there is a clear history of interactions, decisions, and actions taken.

Overcoming Communication Barriers

- **Cultural and Language Differences:** Being mindful of cultural and language differences and seeking to use clear, simple language or translation services when necessary can overcome potential barriers.

- **Resistance to Technology:** Some healthcare professionals may be resistant to new technologies used in communication. Offering training and support can help ease this transition.

- **Information Overload:** Healthcare professionals often juggle numerous responsibilities. Credentialing specialists can help by ensuring communications are necessary, relevant, and succinct.

The Impact of Effective Communication

- **Streamlined Credentialing Processes:** Clear and effective communication can significantly streamline the credentialing process, reducing delays and improving efficiency.

- **Enhanced Relationships:** Building strong, communicative relationships with healthcare professionals fosters a cooperative and supportive environment, essential for successful credentialing.

- **Improved Compliance and Accuracy:** Effective communication ensures that all parties are well-informed about requirements and standards, leading to higher compliance rates and fewer errors in the credentialing process.

Conclusion

Effective communication with healthcare professionals is a foundational skill for credentialing specialists. It not only facilitates the practical aspects of the credentialing process but also builds the trust and respect necessary for successful professional relationships. By prioritizing clear, empathetic, and responsive communication, credentialing specialists can significantly contribute to the efficiency and effectiveness of healthcare services.

8.2. Negotiation and Conflict Resolution

Navigating Challenges in Professional Interactions

In the intricate world of healthcare credentialing, negotiation and conflict resolution are essential skills for credentialing specialists. The credentialing process often involves discussions and decisions that affect the careers of healthcare professionals and the operational dynamics of healthcare institutions. Efficiently managing negotiations and resolving conflicts ensures that these processes contribute positively to the quality and safety of patient care.

Principles of Effective Negotiation

- **Preparation and Research:** Before entering any negotiation, it's crucial to be well-prepared with all relevant information. Understanding both your needs and those of the other party can guide the negotiation towards a mutually beneficial outcome.

- **Clear Communication:** Expressing your position clearly and listening to the other party's needs and concerns lays the foundation for effective negotiation. It's important to articulate the reasons behind your requests or decisions and to understand the motivations of others.

- **Flexibility:** Being open to alternative solutions and compromises can often lead to better outcomes for all parties involved. Flexibility demonstrates a commitment to finding a workable solution rather than winning the argument.

- **Focus on Interests, Not Positions:** Identifying the underlying interests behind the positions taken by each party can reveal common ground and facilitate a resolution that satisfies everyone's core needs.

Strategies for Conflict Resolution

- **Address Conflicts Early:** Addressing conflicts early can prevent them from escalating into larger issues. It's important to recognize when a disagreement is occurring and to approach it proactively.

- **Use a Structured Approach:** Employing a structured approach to conflict resolution, such as the Thomas-Kilmann Conflict Mode Instrument, can help identify the most appropriate strategy for the situation, whether it be collaboration, compromise, accommodation, avoidance, or competition.

- **Seek to Understand Before Being Understood:** Taking the time to listen and understand the other party's perspective without judgment can help de-escalate tensions and pave the way for a resolution.

- **Maintain Professionalism:** Keeping interactions professional and respectful, even in the face of disagreement, preserves the integrity of the relationship and facilitates a more productive resolution process.

The Role of Mediation

In some instances, bringing in a neutral third party to mediate the conflict can be beneficial. Mediators can help facilitate discussions, ensure all voices are heard, and guide the parties towards a mutually acceptable resolution.

Impact of Successful Negotiation and Conflict Resolution

- **Strengthened Professional Relationships:** Successfully navigating negotiations and resolving conflicts can strengthen professional relationships, building trust and respect among colleagues.

- **Improved Credentialing Outcomes:** Effective negotiation and conflict resolution contribute to smoother credentialing processes, ensuring that only qualified professionals are credentialed and that any disputes are resolved fairly and efficiently.

- **Enhanced Organizational Culture:** A culture that values open communication, fair negotiation, and constructive conflict resolution fosters a positive working environment, which can contribute to overall job satisfaction and retention.

Conclusion

Negotiation and conflict resolution are critical competencies for credentialing specialists, enabling them to navigate the complexities of the credentialing process while maintaining positive professional relationships. By applying principles of preparation, clear communication, and flexibility, and by employing effective strategies for resolving disputes, credentialing specialists can contribute significantly to the operational excellence and harmonious environment of healthcare institutions.

8.3. Building Professional Relationships

Foundation of Effective Credentialing

In the healthcare credentialing field, building and maintaining strong professional relationships is not just beneficial; it's essential. The credentialing process involves a network of interactions among credentialing specialists, healthcare providers, administrative staff, and external organizations. These relationships can significantly influence the efficiency, transparency, and success of the credentialing process, ultimately impacting the quality of patient care.

Strategies for Building Professional Relationships

- **Effective Communication:** Clear, consistent, and respectful communication forms the backbone of strong professional relationships. It's important to ensure that all interactions, whether written or verbal, are conducted professionally and considerately.

- **Active Listening:** Demonstrating active listening shows respect for colleagues' opinions and concerns, fostering a culture of mutual respect and collaboration. It involves giving full attention to the speaker, understanding their message, responding appropriately, and remembering the discussion.

- **Reliability and Trustworthiness:** Being reliable and following through on commitments builds trust. Trustworthiness in professional relationships ensures that when credentialing specialists say they will do something, colleagues can depend on them to deliver.

- **Professional Empathy:** Understanding and acknowledging the pressures, challenges, and concerns of healthcare providers and colleagues can strengthen relationships. Empathy involves recognizing the difficult aspects of others' roles and offering support where possible.

- **Networking:** Regularly engaging in professional networking opportunities, such as conferences, seminars, and online forums, can expand your professional circle and foster relationships that may prove beneficial in various aspects of credentialing.

- **Mentorship:** Both seeking mentorship and acting as a mentor can enhance professional relationships. Mentorship provides a framework for sharing knowledge, experiences, and support, contributing to personal and professional growth.

Benefits of Strong Professional Relationships

- **Streamlined Credentialing Processes:** Strong relationships facilitate smoother communication and cooperation among all parties involved in the credentialing process, reducing delays and improving outcomes.

- **Enhanced Problem-Solving:** When challenges or disputes arise, having established relationships can make it easier to find collaborative solutions, as parties are more likely to approach situations with understanding and flexibility.

- **Professional Development:** Relationships built on trust and mutual respect can lead to opportunities for professional development, such as collaborative projects, learning opportunities, and career advancement.

- **Increased Job Satisfaction:** Positive professional relationships contribute to a more supportive and enjoyable work environment, leading to higher job satisfaction and reduced turnover.

Overcoming Challenges

Building professional relationships in the diverse and dynamic environment of healthcare can present challenges, including navigating differences in communication styles, professional boundaries, and time constraints. Overcoming these challenges involves being proactive in communication efforts, setting clear boundaries, and prioritizing relationship-building activities within the constraints of busy schedules.

Conclusion

Building professional relationships is a critical skill for credentialing specialists, underpinning the success of the credentialing process and contributing to a positive work environment. Through effective communication, active listening, reliability, empathy, networking, and mentorship, credentialing specialists can cultivate relationships that not only enhance their professional lives but also positively impact the broader healthcare community.

8.4. Exercise: 10 MCQs with Answers at the End

Creating a set of 10 multiple-choice questions (MCQs) with answers at the end offers a structured way to review and reinforce the concepts discussed in Chapter 8, focusing on "Communication and Interpersonal Skills," particularly in the context of effective communication with healthcare professionals, negotiation and conflict resolution, and building professional relationships. Here are the MCQs designed to encapsulate the key learnings:

Multiple Choice Questions

1. Effective communication in healthcare credentialing is essential for:

   - A) Increasing paperwork

 - B) Ensuring processes are completed efficiently and accurately

   - C) Reducing interaction with healthcare professionals

   - D) Ignoring feedback from colleagues

2. The primary benefit of active listening in professional settings is:

   - A) To minimize the time spent on conversations

   - B) To prevent any meaningful dialogue

- C) To ensure understanding and reduce errors

- D) To dominate discussions with colleagues

3. A professional tone in communication is important because it:

  - A) Limits the clarity of messages

  - B) Fosters respect and facilitates smoother interactions

  - C) Makes conversations more complex

  - D) Discourages open dialogue

4. Flexibility in negotiation refers to:

   - A) Changing your stance frequently to confuse the other party

  - B) Being open to alternative solutions and compromises

  - C) Avoiding any form of agreement

  - D) Sticking rigidly to initial demands

5. A key strategy for building professional relationships is:

  - A) Avoiding all forms of communication

  - B) Active listening and showing empathy

  - C) Keeping professional interactions to a minimum

  - D) Never sharing expertise or insights

6. Reliability and trustworthiness in professional relationships are demonstrated by:

   - A) Regularly missing deadlines

   - B) Making promises that can't be kept

   - C) Following through on commitments

   - D) Withholding information

7. Networking is important for credentialing specialists because it:

   - A) Reduces their workload significantly

   - B) Expands their professional circle and fosters beneficial relationships

   - C) Ensures they work in isolation

   - D) Diminishes their professional reputation

8. Effective conflict resolution in credentialing can lead to:

   - A) Increased misunderstandings among team members

   - B) Strengthened professional relationships

   - C) Decreased trust in the credentialing process

   - D) More frequent conflicts in the future

9. The role of mentorship in professional development includes:

  - A) Limiting career progression opportunities

  - B) Decreasing one's professional network

  - C) Sharing knowledge and experiences

  - D) Encouraging dependency on others

10. Maintaining professionalism in conflict resolution is crucial for:

  - A) Escalating the conflict further

  - B) Preserving the integrity of the relationship and facilitating productive discussions

  - C) Undermining the credibility of colleagues

  - D) Avoiding resolution altogether

Answers

1. B) Ensuring processes are completed efficiently and accurately

2. C) To ensure understanding and reduce errors

3. B) Fosters respect and facilitates smoother interactions

4. B) Being open to alternative solutions and compromises

5. B) Active listening and showing empathy

6. C) Following through on commitments

7. B) Expands their professional circle and fosters beneficial relationships

8. B) Strengthened professional relationships

9. C) Sharing knowledge and experiences

10. B) Preserving the integrity of the relationship and facilitating productive discussions

These questions and answers are designed to reinforce the importance of effective communication, negotiation skills, and the cultivation of professional relationships in the healthcare credentialing process, highlighting the core competencies needed for success in this field.

Chapter 9: Problem-Solving and Critical Thinking

9.1. Analyzing Credentialing Challenges

Identifying and Addressing Complex Issues

Credentialing in healthcare is a multifaceted process that involves verifying the qualifications and backgrounds of healthcare professionals. It is crucial for maintaining the quality and safety of patient care. This process, however, comes with its own set of challenges that require careful analysis and strategic problem-solving. Credentialing specialists must employ critical thinking to navigate these issues effectively, ensuring that the credentialing process is both efficient and rigorous.

Common Credentialing Challenges

- **Incomplete Applications:** One of the most frequent issues is receiving applications from healthcare providers that are incomplete or contain inaccuracies. This can significantly delay the credentialing process.

- **Verification Delays:** Verifying credentials can be time-consuming, especially when awaiting responses from primary sources such as educational institutions, previous employers, or licensing boards.

- **Changing Regulations and Standards:** Healthcare regulations and credentialing standards are continually evolving. Keeping up-to-date with these changes and ensuring compliance can be challenging.

- **Technological Barriers:** The integration of new technology into the credentialing process can improve efficiency but also presents challenges, including data security concerns and the need for training.

Strategies for Analyzing and Addressing Challenges

- **Root Cause Analysis:** Employing techniques such as root cause analysis can help identify the underlying reasons for recurring issues, allowing for more targeted solutions.

- **Process Mapping:** Mapping out the entire credentialing process can highlight inefficiencies and bottlenecks, providing a clear view of where improvements can be made.

- **Stakeholder Engagement:** Involving all stakeholders, including healthcare providers, administrative staff, and IT personnel, in the problem-solving process can ensure that solutions are comprehensive and practical.

- **Continuous Education:** Staying informed about the latest trends, technologies, and regulatory changes in healthcare credentialing can preempt potential challenges.

Implementing Solutions

Once challenges have been analyzed and solutions identified, the next step is implementation. This may involve:

- **Streamlining Application Processes:** Simplifying application forms and providing clear instructions can reduce the incidence of incomplete applications.

- **Leveraging Technology:** Utilizing credentialing software that automates verification processes can significantly reduce delays and improve accuracy.

- **Regular Training and Updates:** Providing regular training sessions for staff on new regulations, standards, and technologies ensures that everyone is equipped to handle the credentialing process effectively.

- **Feedback Loops:** Establishing mechanisms for feedback from healthcare providers and administrative staff can help identify issues early and continuously refine the credentialing process.

The Role of Critical Thinking

Critical thinking is essential throughout the problem-solving process. It involves questioning assumptions, evaluating evidence, and considering alternative solutions. By applying critical thinking, credentialing specialists can develop more effective, innovative solutions to the challenges they face.

Conclusion

Analyzing and addressing credentialing challenges is a dynamic and ongoing process. Through careful analysis, strategic problem-solving, and the application of critical thinking, credentialing specialists can overcome obstacles, streamline operations, and contribute to the overall quality and safety of healthcare services. Implementing thoughtful solutions not only improves the credentialing process but also supports the broader goal of delivering exceptional patient care.

9.2. Strategic Thinking in Credentialing Decisions

Integrating Strategy with Credentialing Processes

Strategic thinking in the context of credentialing decisions involves a forward-looking approach that not only addresses immediate concerns but also anticipates future challenges and opportunities. For credentialing specialists, integrating strategic thinking into their decision-making processes is essential for aligning credentialing practices with the broader goals of healthcare organizations and ensuring the delivery of high-quality patient care.

Elements of Strategic Thinking in Credentialing

- **Alignment with Organizational Goals:** Strategic decisions in credentialing should support the healthcare organization's overall objectives, such as improving patient care, expanding services, or enhancing operational efficiency.

- **Anticipation of Industry Trends:** Keeping abreast of trends in healthcare delivery, technology, and regulations allows credentialing specialists to adapt processes proactively, ensuring that credentialing standards remain relevant and effective.

- **Risk Assessment and Management:** Identifying potential risks, such as changes in licensing requirements or accreditation standards, and developing strategies to mitigate these risks are critical components of strategic thinking.

- **Resource Optimization:** Efficiently allocating resources, including time, personnel, and technology, to the credentialing process ensures that efforts are focused on activities that offer the greatest benefit to the organization.

Applying Strategic Thinking to Credentialing Decisions

- **Scenario Planning:** Engaging in scenario planning can help credentialing specialists anticipate possible future states and develop flexible strategies to address various outcomes.

- **Stakeholder Engagement:** Collaborating with stakeholders, including healthcare providers, administrative staff, and leadership, ensures that credentialing decisions are informed by diverse perspectives and support the needs of all parties involved.

- **Continuous Improvement:** Adopting a mindset of continuous improvement encourages regular evaluation and refinement of credentialing processes, driving efficiency and effectiveness.

- **Leveraging Data and Analytics:** Utilizing data analytics tools to monitor credentialing outcomes and identify patterns can inform strategic decisions, enabling data-driven improvements to credentialing practices.

Challenges to Strategic Thinking in Credentialing

- **Rapidly Changing Healthcare Environment:** The fast pace of change in healthcare can make it difficult to anticipate future trends and requirements, posing a challenge to strategic planning.

- **Resource Constraints:** Limited resources may restrict the ability to implement strategic initiatives, requiring prioritization and creative problem-solving.

- **Resistance to Change:** Organizational inertia and resistance to change among staff or leadership can hinder the adoption of new strategies and innovations in credentialing.

Overcoming Challenges

- **Continuous Learning and Adaptation:** Staying informed about changes in the healthcare landscape and being open to adopting new approaches can help overcome the challenges of a rapidly evolving environment.

- **Effective Communication:** Clear and persuasive communication about the benefits of strategic initiatives can help garner support from stakeholders and overcome resistance to change.

- **Prioritization and Flexibility:** Prioritizing strategic initiatives based on their potential impact and being flexible in their implementation can help manage resource constraints and adapt to unforeseen challenges.

Conclusion

Strategic thinking is vital for credentialing specialists aiming to make decisions that not only address current needs but also position healthcare organizations for future success. By aligning credentialing processes with organizational goals, anticipating industry trends, managing risks, and optimizing resources, credentialing specialists can contribute to the strategic objectives of healthcare organizations, ultimately enhancing the quality of patient care.

9.3. Implementing Solutions

Turning Strategic Insights into Action

In the realm of healthcare credentialing, effectively implementing solutions is as crucial as identifying challenges and devising strategies. This phase is where strategic planning meets practical execution, transforming ideas into tangible improvements in the credentialing process. Successful implementation requires careful planning, coordination, and follow-through to ensure that the solutions not only address the immediate issues but also contribute to the long-term efficiency and effectiveness of credentialing operations.

Steps for Effective Solution Implementation

- **Develop a Detailed Plan:** Begin with a clear, detailed plan that outlines the steps needed to implement the solution, including timelines, responsible parties, and resources required. This plan should also specify the goals and metrics for evaluating the success of the implementation.

- **Engage Stakeholders:** Communication with all stakeholders involved in the credentialing process is vital. Inform them about the planned changes, the rationale behind them, and how they will be affected. Soliciting feedback can also provide valuable insights and foster a sense of ownership among stakeholders.

- **Allocate Resources:** Ensure that the necessary resources, including personnel, technology, and budget, are allocated to support the implementation process. Adequate resourcing is critical for smooth execution and sustainability.

- **Train and Support Staff:** Training sessions and support materials should be provided to staff members who will be directly involved in implementing the new processes or using new systems. Continuous support and open lines of communication are essential for addressing any challenges that arise during the transition.

- **Monitor Progress and Adjust as Needed:** Regular monitoring of the implementation process allows for the tracking of progress against the planned objectives and timelines. Be prepared to make adjustments based on what is learned during the implementation phase. Flexibility can be a valuable asset in dealing with unexpected challenges.

- **Evaluate and Refine:** Once the solution has been implemented, evaluate its effectiveness based on the predefined metrics. Gather feedback from stakeholders and use this information to refine the process further. Continuous improvement should be an integral part of the credentialing process.

Challenges in Implementing Solutions

- **Resistance to Change:** Change can be difficult, and resistance among staff or stakeholders is a common challenge. Addressing concerns directly, providing clear explanations for changes, and demonstrating the benefits can help mitigate resistance.

- **Resource Limitations:** Constraints on time, budget, or personnel can impede the implementation of solutions. Prioritizing resource allocation based on strategic importance and exploring creative solutions can help overcome these limitations.

- **Adapting to Unforeseen Circumstances:** Unexpected issues can arise during implementation, requiring quick thinking and adaptability. Having contingency plans and being prepared to adjust the strategy as needed are crucial for maintaining progress.

Best Practices for Successful Implementation

- **Leadership Support:** Strong support from leadership is critical for successful implementation. Leaders should actively endorse the changes and provide the necessary resources and authority to carry out the plan.

- **Clear Communication:** Keep all stakeholders informed throughout the implementation process. Regular updates, clear documentation, and open forums for questions and feedback can facilitate a smoother transition.

- **Focus on Training and Development:** Comprehensive training programs and ongoing development opportunities for staff are key to ensuring that new processes or technologies are adopted effectively.

Conclusion

Implementing solutions in healthcare credentialing is a dynamic and iterative process that requires careful planning, stakeholder engagement, and continuous evaluation. By effectively managing resources, anticipating challenges, and fostering an environment of open communication and continuous improvement, credentialing specialists can successfully implement solutions that enhance the credentialing process and contribute to the overall quality of healthcare delivery.

9.4. Exercise: 10 MCQs with Answers at the End

Creating a set of 10 multiple-choice questions (MCQs) with answers at the end provides an opportunity to review and reinforce the concepts discussed in Chapter 9, focusing on "Problem-Solving and Critical Thinking," particularly in the context of analyzing credentialing challenges, strategic thinking in credentialing decisions, and implementing solutions. Here are the MCQs designed to encapsulate the key learnings:

Multiple Choice Questions

1. What is a crucial first step in addressing credentialing challenges?

   - A) Ignoring the problem

   - B) Implementing random changes

   - C) Conducting a root cause analysis

   - D) Blaming external factors

2. Strategic thinking in credentialing decisions is primarily aimed at:

   - A) Maintaining the status quo

   - B) Aligning with organizational goals

   - C) Reducing staff numbers

   - D) Increasing paperwork

3. Which of the following is not a strategy for effective solution implementation in credentialing?

   - A) Developing a detailed plan

   - B) Limiting stakeholder communication

   - C) Monitoring progress and adjusting as needed

   - D) Evaluating and refining the process

4. Effective stakeholder engagement during solution implementation involves:

   - A) Keeping plans secret

   - B) Only informing leadership

   - C) Communicating changes and soliciting feedback

   - D) Avoiding any form of feedback

5. A key challenge in implementing credentialing solutions is:

   - A) Excessive resources

   - B) Universal acceptance of change

   - C) Resistance to change

   - D) Lack of challenges

6. When evaluating the effectiveness of implemented solutions, it's important to:

   - A) Ignore stakeholder feedback

   - B) Only consider short-term outcomes

   - C) Use predefined metrics for assessment

   - D) Assume success without evidence

7. Adapting to unforeseen circumstances during implementation requires:

   - A) Rigidity in plans

   - B) Flexibility and contingency planning

   - C) Immediate cessation of the project

   - D) Sole reliance on initial strategies

8. Root cause analysis helps in:

   - A) Complicating simple issues

   - B) Identifying the underlying reasons for challenges

- C) Ignoring the main problem

- D) Increasing operational costs

9. Leadership support in solution implementation is critical for:

  - A) Creating unnecessary bureaucracy

  - B) Providing necessary resources and authority

  - C) Slowing down the process

  - D) Limiting team involvement

10. Continuous improvement in the credentialing process involves:

  - A) Repeating past mistakes

  - B) Never changing procedures

  - C) Regularly evaluating and refining processes

  - D) Avoiding feedback from stakeholders

Answers

1. C) Conducting a root cause analysis

2. B) Aligning with organizational goals

3. B) Limiting stakeholder communication

4. C) Communicating changes and soliciting feedback

5. C) Resistance to change

6. C) Use predefined metrics for assessment

7. B) Flexibility and contingency planning

8. B) Identifying the underlying reasons for challenges

9. B) Providing necessary resources and authority

10. C) Regularly evaluating and refining processes

These questions and answers are designed to reinforce the critical aspects of problem-solving and critical thinking in the credentialing process, highlighting the importance of strategic planning, effective implementation, and continuous improvement.

Chapter 10: Credentialing for Telemedicine

10.1. Unique Aspects of Telemedicine Credentialing

Adapting Credentialing to the Digital Age

Telemedicine has revolutionized the way healthcare is delivered, offering patients remote access to medical services. This shift towards digital health requires a reevaluation of traditional credentialing processes to address the unique challenges and opportunities presented by telemedicine. Credentialing for telemedicine involves verifying the qualifications of healthcare providers who deliver care remotely, ensuring they meet all regulatory, legal, and professional standards.

Key Differences in Telemedicine Credentialing

- **Cross-Jurisdictional Licensing:** Telemedicine often involves providing care to patients in different states or regions from where the provider is located. Credentialing must therefore ensure that providers are licensed and authorized to practice in the patient's location, which may involve obtaining multiple state licenses or special telehealth licenses.

- **Technology Proficiency:** Credentialing for telemedicine must assess a provider's competency with the technology platforms used to deliver care remotely. This includes not just the ability to use telemedicine software but also an understanding of best practices for virtual patient interaction and maintaining privacy and security.

- **Quality Assurance in a Remote Setting:** Ensuring the quality of care delivered remotely poses unique challenges. Credentialing processes must include mechanisms to assess and monitor the quality of telehealth services, such as patient satisfaction, adherence to telehealth protocols, and outcome measures.

- **Privacy and Security Compliance:** Telemedicine involves the transmission of sensitive patient information over digital platforms. Credentialing must verify that providers understand and comply with all relevant privacy and security regulations, including HIPAA in the United States, to protect patient information.

Strategies for Effective Telemedicine Credentialing

- **Collaboration with Regulatory Bodies:** Working closely with state medical boards and other regulatory agencies can help navigate the complex landscape of telehealth regulations and ensure compliance.

- **Utilization of Telehealth Credentialing Consortia:** Joining consortia or networks that facilitate the credentialing of telehealth providers across state lines can streamline the process and reduce administrative burdens.

- **Ongoing Education and Training:** Providing telehealth providers with continuous education on the latest telemedicine technologies, best practices, and legal requirements is essential for maintaining high standards of care.

- **Robust Technology Assessment:** Credentialing processes should include a thorough assessment of the telemedicine platforms used by providers, ensuring they meet technical and security standards.

Challenges and Considerations

- **Rapidly Changing Regulations:** The legal landscape for telehealth is evolving rapidly, making it challenging to stay up-to-date with the latest regulations across different jurisdictions.

- **Interstate Practice Complications:** The need for providers to be credentialed in multiple states can create administrative challenges and potentially limit access to telehealth services in areas with provider shortages.

- **Ensuring Equivalency of Care:** Credentialing must ensure that the standard of care delivered via telemedicine is equivalent to that of in-person services, addressing any disparities in access or quality.

Conclusion

Credentialing for telemedicine presents unique challenges that require a tailored approach, reflecting the specific demands of delivering healthcare remotely. By addressing these challenges head-on—through careful planning, collaboration, and ongoing education—credentialing bodies can ensure that telemedicine services are provided by qualified, competent professionals, thereby extending the reach of high-quality healthcare to patients, regardless of their location.

10.2. Regulatory Considerations

Navigating the Legal Landscape of Telemedicine

The expansion of telemedicine services has brought regulatory considerations to the forefront of the credentialing process. These regulations are designed to ensure that telehealth services are provided safely, securely, and in a manner that protects patient privacy. Credentialing specialists must navigate a complex web of federal, state, and international regulations to ensure compliance and maintain the integrity of telemedicine practices.

Key Regulatory Areas in Telemedicine Credentialing

- **Licensure and Cross-State Practice:** One of the primary regulatory considerations is the requirement that healthcare providers are licensed in the state where the patient is located. Some states participate in interstate licensure compacts that facilitate cross-state practice, but credentialing specialists must verify state-specific requirements.

- **Privacy and Security Regulations:** Telemedicine involves the electronic transmission of health information, making compliance with privacy and security regulations, such as the Health Insurance Portability and Accountability Act (HIPAA) in the United States, crucial. Credentialing must ensure that providers understand and adhere to these regulations to protect patient data.

- **Telehealth Reimbursement Policies:** Reimbursement for telemedicine services varies by state and insurer. Credentialing specialists need to be aware of the reimbursement policies of different insurance providers and Medicare/Medicaid to ensure that telemedicine services are covered.

- **Quality of Care Standards:** Regulatory bodies have established standards to ensure that the quality of care provided through telemedicine is equivalent to that of in-person services. Credentialing processes must assess providers' ability to meet these standards, including their proficiency in using telemedicine technologies and following clinical guidelines.

Strategies for Addressing Regulatory Considerations

- **Staying Informed:** Keeping up-to-date with the latest regulatory changes is essential. Credentialing specialists can subscribe to updates from regulatory agencies, professional associations, and legal resources specializing in healthcare law.

- **Educating Providers:** Part of the credentialing process should involve educating providers on the regulatory requirements relevant to telemedicine, including licensure, privacy, security, and quality of care.

- **Leveraging Technology:** Utilizing credentialing software that includes regulatory compliance features can help manage the complexities of telemedicine regulations, ensuring that all providers meet the necessary standards.

- **Collaboration with Legal Experts:** Collaborating with legal experts who specialize in telehealth can provide valuable insights into regulatory compliance and help navigate the legal aspects of cross-state licensure and international practice.

Challenges in Regulatory Compliance

- **Evolving Regulations:** The rapid evolution of telehealth regulations can make compliance challenging. Credentialing specialists must be proactive in monitoring for changes and adapting processes accordingly.

- **Interstate Licensure:** The requirement for licensure in the patient's state poses logistical challenges, especially in regions with varying regulations. Interstate compacts and emergency licensure waivers during public health emergencies are strategies to address this issue.

- **Technology Standards:** Ensuring that telemedicine platforms comply with technical and security standards requires ongoing vigilance and cooperation with IT departments and vendors.

Conclusion

Regulatory considerations are a critical component of the credentialing process for telemedicine, requiring a comprehensive understanding of the legal requirements governing telehealth services. By adopting proactive strategies to stay informed, educating providers, leveraging technology, and collaborating with legal experts, credentialing specialists can ensure compliance with these regulations, thereby supporting the safe and effective delivery of telemedicine services.

10.3. Ensuring Provider Competency in Telemedicine

Maintaining High Standards in Remote Healthcare Delivery

As telemedicine continues to grow, ensuring that providers are competent in delivering high-quality remote healthcare services is paramount. This competency goes beyond traditional medical expertise, encompassing technical proficiency, effective online communication skills, and a thorough understanding of telehealth protocols. Credentialing processes play a crucial role in assessing and maintaining these competencies, safeguarding patient care in the digital healthcare environment.

Key Competencies for Telemedicine Providers

- **Clinical Skills for Remote Care:** Providers must demonstrate the ability to diagnose, treat, and manage patients remotely, adapting clinical practices to the telemedicine context while maintaining the standard of care equivalent to in-person visits.

- **Technical Proficiency:** Competency in using telehealth platforms and technology is essential. Providers should be able to troubleshoot basic technical issues and ensure a smooth and secure virtual visit for patients.

- **Communication Skills:** Effective communication in a virtual setting requires clear articulation, the ability to build rapport with patients remotely, and the use of visual cues to assess and respond to patient needs and concerns.

- **Privacy and Security Awareness:** Providers must be knowledgeable about and comply with laws and regulations regarding patient privacy and data security, including the proper handling of electronic health records and secure communication with patients.

- **Cultural Competency:** Delivering care to a diverse patient population via telemedicine requires sensitivity to cultural differences and an understanding of how these may impact patient care and communication.

Strategies for Ensuring Competency

- **Credentialing and Training Programs:** Credentialing processes should include specific criteria and training programs focused on telemedicine competencies. These programs can cover technical training, best practices for virtual patient engagement, and legal requirements for telehealth.

- **Continuous Professional Development:** Encouraging ongoing education and professional development in telemedicine can help providers stay current with emerging technologies, clinical guidelines, and regulatory changes affecting telehealth.

- **Performance Monitoring:** Implementing mechanisms to monitor and evaluate the quality of telemedicine services, such as patient satisfaction surveys, peer reviews, and outcome tracking, can provide feedback on provider competency and areas for improvement.

- **Collaboration and Support:** Fostering a culture of collaboration among telemedicine providers, including opportunities for mentorship and peer support, can enhance learning and competency in telehealth practices.

Challenges in Ensuring Telemedicine Competency

- **Adapting to Rapid Technological Changes:** The fast pace of technological advancement in telehealth can make it challenging for providers to remain proficient with new tools and platforms.

- **Assessing Competency Remotely:** Evaluating the competencies of telemedicine providers remotely poses unique challenges, requiring innovative approaches to credentialing and performance assessment.

- **Ensuring Equitable Access to Training:** Access to telemedicine training and resources may vary, potentially leading to disparities in provider competency. Credentialing bodies must ensure that all providers have the opportunity to acquire and maintain the necessary skills.

Conclusion

Ensuring provider competency in telemedicine is a multi-faceted challenge that requires a comprehensive approach to credentialing, training, and ongoing professional development. By establishing clear competency criteria, providing access to training, monitoring performance, and fostering a supportive professional community, credentialing bodies can help maintain the high standards of care that patients expect and deserve in the telehealth setting. This commitment to competency not only enhances the quality of telemedicine services but also supports the broader integration of telehealth into the healthcare system.

10.4. Exercise: 10 MCQs with Answers at the End

Creating a set of 10 multiple-choice questions (MCQs) with answers at the end provides an effective way to review and reinforce the concepts discussed in Chapter 10, focusing on "Credentialing for Telemedicine," particularly in the unique aspects of telemedicine credentialing, regulatory considerations, and ensuring provider competency in telemedicine. Here are the MCQs designed to encapsulate the key learnings:

Multiple Choice Questions

1. Telemedicine credentialing must uniquely address:

   - A) Only the provider's in-person clinical skills.

- B) The provider's ability to use telehealth platforms effectively.

   - C) The physical location of the telemedicine equipment.

   - D) The provider's preference for telemedicine over in-person care.

2. Cross-jurisdictional licensing in telemedicine is important because:

   - A) It allows providers to practice in any country without restriction.

   - B) Providers must be licensed in the state where the patient is located.

   - C) All medical licenses are universally accepted.

   - D) It eliminates the need for credentialing.

3. A critical aspect of telemedicine competency is:

   - A) Avoiding the use of technology.

   - B) Effective online communication skills.

   - C) Preferring traditional methods over telehealth.

   - D) Limiting access to telehealth services.

4. Privacy and security awareness in telemedicine involves understanding:

   - A) Only the provider's personal information security.

   - B) Laws and regulations regarding patient privacy and data security.

   - C) The importance of public sharing of patient data.

   - D) Avoiding electronic health records.

5. Continuous professional development in telemedicine is necessary due to:

   - A) The unchanging nature of telehealth technology.

   - B) Decreasing legal requirements and regulations.

   - C) Emerging technologies and clinical guidelines.

   - D) The lack of patient interest in telehealth.

6. Performance monitoring in telemedicine can include:

   - A) Ignoring patient feedback.

   - B) Patient satisfaction surveys and outcome tracking.

   - C) Solely focusing on the number of telehealth visits.

   - D) Discouraging peer reviews.

7. Challenges in ensuring telemedicine competency include:

   - A) The static pace of technological advancement.

   - B) Easy assessment of competencies remotely.

   - C) Rapid technological changes.

   - D) Universal access to comprehensive training.

8. Regulatory considerations in telemedicine credentialing do not include:

   - A) Adherence to local food and drug regulations.

   - B) Compliance with privacy and security regulations.

   - C) Licensure and cross-state practice regulations.

   - D) Telehealth reimbursement policies.

9. Key strategies for addressing regulatory considerations in telemedicine include:

   - A) Avoiding updates on regulations.

   - B) Staying informed about regulatory changes.

   - C) Limiting stakeholder communication.

   - D) Reducing the use of technology in care delivery.

10. Ensuring equitable access to telemedicine training and resources addresses the challenge of:

   - A) Overabundance of resources.

   - B) Disparities in provider competency.

   - C) Uniform technological advancements.

   - D) Excessive regulatory oversight.

Answers

1. B) The provider's ability to use telehealth platforms effectively.

2. B) Providers must be licensed in the state where the patient is located.

3. B) Effective online communication skills.

4. B) Laws and regulations regarding patient privacy and data security.

5. C) Emerging technologies and clinical guidelines.

6. B) Patient satisfaction surveys and outcome tracking.

7. C) Rapid technological changes.

8. A) Adherence to local food and drug regulations.

9. B) Staying informed about regulatory changes.

10. B) Disparities in provider competency.

These questions and answers are designed to reinforce the importance of adapting credentialing processes for telemedicine, understanding regulatory frameworks, and ensuring that providers are competent in delivering high-quality remote healthcare services.

Chapter 11: Quality Improvement in Credentialing

11.1. Identifying Areas for Improvement

Foundational Steps for Enhancing Credentialing Processes

In the realm of healthcare, continuous quality improvement (CQI) in credentialing processes is vital to ensuring that healthcare providers meet the highest standards of care and compliance. Identifying areas for improvement within credentialing practices is the first critical step in this ongoing journey towards excellence. This process involves systematic evaluation, feedback collection, and data analysis to pinpoint inefficiencies, inaccuracies, or areas that may benefit from modernization or enhanced protocols.

Key Strategies for Identification

- **Data Analysis and Benchmarking:** Utilize data analytics to monitor credentialing timelines, error rates, and compliance issues. Comparing these metrics against industry benchmarks can highlight areas lagging behind best practices.

- **Feedback Loops:** Implement structured feedback mechanisms from both internal teams (credentialing staff, administration) and external stakeholders (healthcare providers, accreditation bodies). This feedback is invaluable in identifying pain points and areas needing clarity or streamlining.

- **Process Mapping:** Visually mapping out the entire credentialing process can reveal redundancies, unnecessary complexities, or bottlenecks that hinder efficiency and effectiveness.

- **Regulatory and Compliance Reviews:** Regular reviews of changes in healthcare regulations and compliance standards can identify areas where the credentialing process needs updates to stay aligned with legal requirements.

- **Technology Utilization Assessment:** Assessing the current use of technology within the credentialing process can identify opportunities for automation or digital solutions to replace manual, time-consuming tasks.

Areas Commonly Identified for Improvement

- **Application and Documentation Processes:** Simplifying application forms, reducing paperwork, and ensuring clear instructions can enhance the submission process for healthcare providers.

- **Verification and Background Check Efficiency:** Streamlining verification procedures through automation or enhanced protocols can reduce turnaround times and improve accuracy.

- **Communication Channels:** Establishing clear, effective communication channels between credentialing teams and providers ensures timely updates and reduces misunderstandings.

- **Training and Development:** Identifying gaps in staff training, particularly regarding changes in regulations or new technology, can improve the credentialing team's competency and effectiveness.

- **Policy and Procedure Updates:** Regularly updating policies and procedures to reflect current best practices and regulatory requirements ensures the credentialing process remains relevant and compliant.

Implementing Changes for Improvement

Once areas for improvement have been identified, the next steps involve prioritizing these areas based on impact, feasibility, and resources required. Developing a structured plan for implementing changes, including setting timelines, allocating resources, and defining success metrics, is crucial for tangible improvements.

Conclusion

Identifying areas for improvement within credentialing processes is a proactive approach to enhancing the quality and efficiency of healthcare provider verification and compliance. By employing strategic data analysis, soliciting feedback, and engaging in continuous process evaluation, credentialing departments can ensure their practices not only meet but exceed the standards required for high-quality patient care. This ongoing commitment to quality improvement supports the foundational goal of credentialing: to uphold the safety, competence, and integrity of healthcare delivery.

11.2. Implementing Quality Improvement Initiatives

Transforming Insight into Action

After identifying areas for improvement in the credentialing process, the next critical step involves the strategic implementation of quality improvement (QI) initiatives. This phase is where planning meets execution, and theoretical improvements are applied in practical settings to enhance the credentialing process's efficiency, accuracy, and compliance.

Successful implementation requires a structured approach, clear communication, and ongoing monitoring to ensure that the initiatives achieve the intended outcomes.

Strategies for Effective Implementation

- **Prioritization of Initiatives:** Begin by prioritizing identified improvements based on their potential impact on the credentialing process, resource requirements, and urgency. This helps in focusing efforts on areas that will provide the most significant benefits.

- **Development of Action Plans:** For each initiative, develop a detailed action plan outlining the steps needed for implementation, including timelines, responsible parties, resource allocation, and performance metrics for evaluating success.

- **Stakeholder Engagement:** Engage all relevant stakeholders early in the process, including credentialing staff, healthcare providers, IT personnel, and leadership. Their input and buy-in are crucial for smooth implementation and long-term sustainability.

- **Training and Education:** Provide comprehensive training and education for all individuals involved in the implementation of new processes or technologies. Ensuring that staff are well-prepared and confident in their roles is essential for the success of QI initiatives.

- **Phased Roll-Out:** Consider implementing new initiatives in phases, allowing for the testing of changes in a controlled environment before full-scale implementation. This approach can help identify potential issues and make necessary adjustments before broader application.

- **Monitoring and Feedback:** Establish mechanisms for continuous monitoring of the implementation process and collection of feedback from stakeholders. Regular reviews allow for the assessment of progress and the identification of areas needing further adjustment.

Common Challenges and Solutions

- **Resistance to Change:** Change can be met with resistance. Addressing concerns directly, providing clear rationales for changes, and demonstrating the benefits can help mitigate resistance.

- **Resource Constraints:** Limited resources may hinder the implementation of QI initiatives. Prioritizing initiatives and seeking creative solutions, such as leveraging existing resources or identifying new funding sources, can address this challenge.

- **Maintaining Momentum:** Keeping the momentum going for QI initiatives can be difficult, especially with competing priorities. Regular updates, celebrating milestones, and visible leadership support can maintain focus and enthusiasm.

Measuring Success

- **Establish Clear Metrics:** Define clear, measurable metrics for each QI initiative at the outset. These could include reduction in credentialing times, decrease in errors, or improvements in provider satisfaction.

- **Regular Evaluation:** Conduct regular evaluations against these metrics to assess the impact of the QI initiatives. Use this data to refine processes further and to demonstrate the value of the initiatives to stakeholders.

- **Adaptation and Continuous Improvement:** Be prepared to adapt initiatives based on performance data and feedback. Continuous improvement should be an integral part of the credentialing process, with lessons learned informing future QI efforts.

Conclusion

Implementing quality improvement initiatives in credentialing is a dynamic process that requires careful planning, stakeholder engagement, and continuous monitoring. By approaching implementation with a structured methodology, addressing potential challenges proactively, and measuring success through clear metrics, credentialing departments can significantly enhance the quality and effectiveness of their processes. This commitment to improvement not only optimizes credentialing operations but also contributes to the overarching goal of ensuring high-quality patient care through the verification of healthcare provider qualifications and competencies.

11.3. Measuring Success in Credentialing Processes

Establishing Benchmarks for Continuous Improvement

Measuring success in credentialing processes is crucial for ensuring that healthcare providers are qualified and capable of delivering high-quality patient care. It involves setting clear benchmarks, utilizing data-driven metrics, and regularly reviewing outcomes to identify areas for continuous improvement. By effectively measuring success, credentialing departments can enhance operational efficiency, ensure compliance with regulatory standards, and contribute to the overall quality of healthcare services.

Key Metrics for Measuring Success

- **Time to Credential:** This metric tracks the average time taken to complete the credentialing process for a provider. Reducing this time, without compromising the thoroughness of the process, indicates increased efficiency.

- **Application Accuracy Rate:** Measures the percentage of applications completed accurately and fully on the first submission. A high accuracy rate suggests clear communication and effective guidance for applicants.

- **Compliance Rate:** Tracks adherence to regulatory and accreditation standards within the credentialing process. High compliance rates indicate success in meeting or exceeding industry standards.

- **Provider Satisfaction:** Assesses the satisfaction of healthcare providers with the credentialing process. Surveys can gauge perceptions of efficiency, communication, and overall ease of the process.

- **Error Rate:** Identifies the frequency of errors or discrepancies in the credentialing documentation and verification process. A low error rate signifies high accuracy and reliability.

Strategies for Effective Measurement

- **Implementing Credentialing Software:** Utilizing specialized software can automate data collection and reporting, providing real-time access to key metrics and trends.

- **Regular Audits:** Conducting regular audits of the credentialing process can help verify the accuracy of records, ensure compliance, and identify areas for improvement.

- **Stakeholder Feedback:** Collecting and analyzing feedback from both internal and external stakeholders, including healthcare providers and administrative staff, can provide insights into the effectiveness of the credentialing process.

- **Benchmarking:** Comparing performance metrics against industry benchmarks or historical data can help credentialing departments understand their relative performance and set realistic improvement goals.

Challenges in Measuring Success

- **Data Integrity:** Ensuring the accuracy and completeness of the data used for measurement can be challenging. Regular data validation processes are necessary to maintain integrity.

- **Changing Standards and Regulations:** The dynamic nature of healthcare regulations and standards requires that credentialing departments continuously update their measurement criteria to remain relevant.

- **Resource Limitations:** Limited resources, including staffing and technology, can impact the ability to measure and analyze success effectively. Prioritizing investments in key areas is essential for overcoming this challenge.

Utilizing Success Metrics for Improvement

- **Actionable Insights:** Use the data collected to develop actionable insights for improving the credentialing process. This could involve streamlining documentation requirements, enhancing training for staff, or implementing new technologies.

- **Continuous Feedback Loop:** Establish a continuous feedback loop where insights and improvements are regularly reviewed and adjusted based on new data and stakeholder feedback.

- **Celebrating Successes:** Recognizing and celebrating improvements in credentialing processes can motivate staff and reinforce the value of continuous improvement efforts.

Conclusion

Measuring success in credentialing processes is a critical component of ensuring high-quality healthcare delivery. By leveraging key metrics, engaging with stakeholders, and utilizing data for continuous improvement, credentialing departments can enhance their operations, support healthcare providers, and ultimately contribute to better patient care outcomes. This ongoing commitment to excellence and improvement underscores the vital role of credentialing in the healthcare ecosystem.

11.4. Exercise: 10 MCQs with Answers at the End

Creating a set of 10 multiple-choice questions (MCQs) with answers at the end offers a comprehensive way to review and reinforce the concepts discussed in Chapter 11, focusing on "Quality Improvement in Credentialing," particularly around identifying areas for improvement, implementing quality improvement initiatives, and measuring success in credentialing processes. Here are the MCQs designed to encapsulate the key learnings:

Multiple Choice Questions

1. What is a primary goal of quality improvement in credentialing?

   - A) To increase the paperwork involved in the process

   - B) To ensure healthcare providers meet the highest standards of care

   - C) To discourage new providers from applying

   - D) To complicate the credentialing process

2. Which metric is crucial for measuring the efficiency of the credentialing process?

   - A) Time to Credential

   - B) Color of the application form

- C) Number of coffee breaks taken by staff

- D) Office temperature

3. A high application accuracy rate indicates:

  - A) The need for more training

  - B) Clear communication and effective guidance for applicants

  - C) A lack of attention to detail

  - D) That applications are too simple

4. Regular audits of the credentialing process help in:

  - A) Increasing errors in documentation

  - B) Verifying the accuracy of records and ensuring compliance

  - C) Slowing down the process

  - D) Discouraging feedback

5. Provider satisfaction as a metric is important because:

  - A) It ensures the process is inconvenient

  - B) It assesses the providers' perception of the credentialing efficiency and communication

  - C) It is unrelated to the credentialing process

  - D) Providers prefer complicated processes

6. The implementation of credentialing software primarily helps to:

   - A) Decrease data accuracy

   - B) Automate data collection and reporting

   - C) Make the process more manual

   - D) Increase the credentialing timeline

7. Benchmarking in the credentialing process is used to:

   - A) Ignore industry standards

   - B) Compare performance metrics against industry benchmarks or historical data

   - C) Decrease organizational transparency

   - D) Reduce staff motivation

8. A challenge in measuring success in credentialing is:

   - A) Too few regulations and standards

   - B) The dynamic nature of healthcare regulations and standards

   - C) An overabundance of resources

   - D) Stakeholders' unanimous agreement

9. Utilizing success metrics for improvement involves:

   - A) Ignoring the data collected

   - B) Developing actionable insights for process enhancement

- C) Maintaining the status quo

- D) Decreasing stakeholder engagement

10. Continuous feedback loops in credentialing are important for:

- A) Repeating past mistakes

- B) Regularly reviewing and adjusting improvements based on new data

- C) Eliminating all forms of feedback

- D) Ensuring the process never changes

Answers

1. B) To ensure healthcare providers meet the highest standards of care

2. A) Time to Credential

3. B) Clear communication and effective guidance for applicants

4. B) Verifying the accuracy of records and ensuring compliance

5. B) It assesses the providers' perception of the credentialing efficiency and communication

6. B) Automate data collection and reporting

7. B) Compare performance metrics against industry benchmarks or historical data

8. B) The dynamic nature of healthcare regulations and standards

9. B) Developing actionable insights for process enhancement

10. B) Regularly reviewing and adjusting improvements based on new data

These questions and answers are designed to reinforce the importance of continuous quality improvement in the credentialing process, highlighting key strategies for identifying areas for improvement, effectively implementing initiatives, and measuring success to enhance the overall quality of healthcare services.

Chapter 12: Credentialing and Provider Enrollment

12.1. The Link Between Credentialing and Enrollment

Integrating Credentialing with Provider Enrollment

In the healthcare industry, the processes of credentialing and provider enrollment are closely interconnected, forming a critical pathway that ensures healthcare providers are not only qualified but also authorized to bill insurance companies for their services. While credentialing verifies the qualifications, training, and experience of healthcare providers, provider enrollment is the process by which providers are formally added to health insurance networks, allowing them to receive payment for services rendered to insured patients.

Understanding the Relationship

- **Credentialing as a Prerequisite:** Credentialing is typically the first step in the pathway. Providers must successfully complete the credentialing process, proving their qualifications and competency, before they can proceed to enrollment with insurance companies.

- **Enrollment for Reimbursement:** Once credentialed, providers undergo the enrollment process with various insurers, including Medicare and Medicaid, to become in-network providers. This step is crucial for the financial viability of both the providers and the healthcare organizations they represent, as it directly impacts reimbursement for patient care services.

- **Quality and Compliance Assurance:** Both processes serve to assure quality and compliance within the healthcare system. Credentialing ensures that providers meet specific standards of professional practice, while enrollment establishes that these providers are eligible to offer services under insurance plans, adhering to the contractual and regulatory requirements of insurers.

Challenges in Linking Credentialing and Enrollment

- **Time-Consuming Processes:** Both credentialing and enrollment can be lengthy, often taking several months to complete. Delays in either process can hinder providers' ability to deliver care and receive timely reimbursement.

- **Varying Requirements:** Insurance companies may have different requirements and documentation for enrollment, adding complexity to the process and potentially leading to confusion or errors.

- **Regulatory and Policy Changes:** Frequent changes in healthcare regulations and insurance policies can impact credentialing and enrollment processes, requiring constant vigilance and adaptability from healthcare organizations.

Strategies for Effective Integration

- **Streamlining Processes:** Developing integrated systems and workflows that streamline both credentialing and enrollment can reduce duplication of effort and minimize delays.

- **Technology Utilization:** Leveraging technology, such as provider credentialing and enrollment software, can automate many aspects of the processes, improving efficiency and accuracy.

- **Regular Communication:** Establishing regular communication channels between credentialing teams, providers, and insurance companies ensures that any issues are promptly addressed and that everyone is informed of the status of credentialing and enrollment.

- **Continuous Training and Education:** Providing ongoing training for credentialing staff on the latest regulatory requirements, insurance policies, and best practices can help navigate the complexities of linking credentialing and enrollment.

Conclusion

The link between credentialing and provider enrollment is fundamental to the functioning of the healthcare system, impacting both the quality of patient care and the financial sustainability of healthcare services. By understanding and effectively managing this relationship, healthcare organizations can ensure that providers are qualified, compliant, and appropriately reimbursed for their services. Implementing strategies to streamline and integrate these processes can lead to more efficient operations, satisfied providers, and ultimately, better patient outcomes.

12.2. Navigating the Enrollment Process

Streamlining Access to Insurance Networks

The enrollment process is a critical step for healthcare providers seeking to join insurance networks and obtain reimbursement for services rendered to insured patients. Successfully navigating this process requires an understanding of insurance companies' requirements, timely submission of accurate documentation, and regular follow-up. This step is essential not only for the financial viability of healthcare providers but also for ensuring that patients have access to a broad range of in-network healthcare services.

Key Steps in the Enrollment Process

- **Understanding Insurer Requirements:** Each insurance company has its own set of requirements for provider enrollment. These can include specific forms, documentation of credentials, and proof of liability insurance. Understanding these requirements upfront can help avoid delays.

- **Accurate and Complete Application Submission:** Submitting a complete and accurate application is crucial. This includes ensuring that all required documentation is up to date and correctly filled out. Inaccuracies or omissions can lead to significant delays in the enrollment process.

- **Follow-up and Communication:** Regular follow-up with the insurance company after submitting the enrollment application is essential to track progress and address any issues or additional information requests promptly.

- **Credentialing Verification:** Many insurers conduct their own credentialing verification process as part of enrollment. Providers should be prepared to supply any additional information required and respond to queries in a timely manner.

Challenges in the Enrollment Process

- **Complexity and Variability:** The enrollment process can vary significantly between insurers, adding complexity and the potential for confusion among providers trying to enroll with multiple networks.

- **Regulatory Changes:** Changes in healthcare regulations can impact enrollment requirements and processes, necessitating continuous monitoring and adaptation by healthcare providers and their administrative staff.

- **Delays in Processing:** Delays in processing enrollment applications can impede providers' ability to deliver care to patients covered by specific insurance plans, affecting both patient access and provider revenue.

Strategies for Successful Enrollment

- **Centralized Enrollment Management:** Utilizing centralized systems or software for managing enrollment applications can help streamline the process, track progress with various insurers, and ensure timely submission of documentation.

- **Regular Training:** Providing regular training for staff involved in the enrollment process on changes in insurance requirements and best practices can enhance efficiency and accuracy.

- **Engagement with Payer Relations:** Developing strong relationships with payer relations representatives can provide valuable insights into specific insurer requirements and facilitate smoother communication during the enrollment process.

- **Leveraging Professional Assistance:** For some healthcare providers, especially smaller practices or those new to the process, seeking assistance from professional enrollment services or consultants can be a valuable strategy for navigating the complexities of enrollment with multiple insurers.

Conclusion

Navigating the provider enrollment process is a critical component of ensuring access to insurance networks and securing reimbursement for healthcare services. By understanding the key steps and challenges involved, and by implementing effective strategies for managing the process, healthcare providers can improve their operational efficiency, enhance patient access to care, and maintain financial stability. Continuous engagement with the process, adaptation to regulatory changes, and effective communication with insurance companies are essential for successful enrollment.

12.3. Overcoming Enrollment Challenges

Strategies for Smoothing the Path to Insurance Network Participation

Provider enrollment in insurance networks is fraught with challenges that can delay or even prevent healthcare providers from serving insured patients. These challenges range from navigating the diverse requirements of different insurers to managing the complex documentation needed for the application process. Overcoming these hurdles is crucial for ensuring that providers can offer their services to a broader patient base and secure reimbursement for their care. Here are strategies to address and overcome common enrollment challenges:

Understanding and Anticipating Common Challenges

- **Varying Requirements Across Insurers:** Insurance companies may have different processes, documentation requirements, and timelines for enrollment.

- **Delays in Processing Applications:** Lengthy processing times can lead to frustration and may impact the provider's ability to deliver timely care to patients.

- **Documentation Errors and Omissions:** Incomplete or inaccurate applications are a significant source of delays in the enrollment process.

- **Keeping Up with Regulatory Changes:** Frequent changes in healthcare regulations and insurance policies can complicate the enrollment process.

Strategies for Overcoming Challenges

- **Thorough Preparation and Research:** Start by gathering all necessary information and understanding the specific requirements of each insurer with whom you plan to enroll. This upfront investment can significantly reduce delays and rejections.

- **Leverage Technology:** Utilize provider enrollment and credentialing software that can help organize, track, and manage the application process for multiple insurers. These tools can also alert you to deadlines and missing information.

- **Establish Direct Communication Lines:** Develop relationships with representatives from insurance companies. Having a direct point of contact can facilitate smoother communication, quicker resolution of issues, and provide insights into common pitfalls to avoid.

- **Regular Follow-up:** Proactively follow up on submitted applications to check their status and respond promptly to any requests for additional information or clarification. Regular follow-ups can help keep your application moving through the process.

- **Training and Continuous Education:** Ensure that staff responsible for enrollment are trained and kept up-to-date with the latest insurance regulations, documentation practices, and industry trends. Continuous education can help mitigate the risk of errors and improve the efficiency of the enrollment process.

- **Seek Professional Assistance:** For practices facing significant challenges or lacking the resources to manage the enrollment process effectively, consulting with professional enrollment services or specialists can provide the expertise needed to navigate complex requirements and expedite enrollment.

Implementing Best Practices

- **Documentation Accuracy:** Double-check applications for completeness and accuracy before submission. Consider implementing a checklist system to ensure all necessary documentation is included.

- **Streamlined Internal Processes:** Develop clear, streamlined internal processes for gathering, reviewing, and submitting enrollment documentation. Standardizing these processes can reduce errors and inefficiencies.

- **Adaptability:** Be prepared to adapt processes in response to feedback from insurers and changes in regulatory requirements. Flexibility and a willingness to adjust strategies as needed are key to overcoming enrollment challenges.

Conclusion

Overcoming enrollment challenges requires a proactive, informed approach that prioritizes thorough preparation, effective communication, and the strategic use of technology. By adopting these strategies, healthcare providers can navigate the complexities of the enrollment process more smoothly, ensuring timely access to insurance networks and improving their ability to deliver care to a wider range of patients. Continuous improvement and adaptation to changing requirements and challenges are essential for maintaining successful enrollment in insurance networks.

12.4. Exercise: 10 MCQs with Answers at the End

Creating a set of 10 multiple-choice questions (MCQs) with answers at the end provides a structured way to review and reinforce the concepts discussed in Chapter 12, focusing on "Credentialing and Provider Enrollment," particularly around the link between credentialing and enrollment, navigating the enrollment process, and overcoming enrollment challenges. Here are the MCQs designed to encapsulate the key learnings:

Multiple Choice Questions

1. Credentialing must be completed **before** which of the following steps?

   - A) Hiring a healthcare provider

   - B) Provider enrollment with insurance companies

   - C) Graduating from medical school

   - D) Starting a healthcare facility

2. What is a primary goal of provider enrollment?

   - A) To limit the number of patients a provider can see

   - B) To allow providers to bill insurance companies for services rendered

   - C) To increase paperwork for healthcare providers

   - D) To discourage providers from joining new practices

3. A significant challenge in the provider enrollment process is:

   - A) Too rapid processing of applications

   - B) Uniform requirements across all insurers

   - C) Varying requirements across different insurers

   - D) Lack of necessary documentation for healthcare providers

4. Effective strategies to navigate enrollment challenges include all except:

   - A) Ignoring communications from insurance companies

   - B) Leveraging technology to manage the process

   - C) Establishing direct communication lines with insurers

   - D) Regular follow-up on submitted applications

5. The use of provider enrollment and credentialing software can primarily help in:

   - A) Decreasing efficiency

   - B) Organizing and tracking the application process

   - C) Increasing the likelihood of application denial

   - D) Reducing direct communication with insurance companies

6. Regular training for staff involved in enrollment processes is crucial for:

   - A) Keeping up with regulatory changes and documentation practices

   - B) Increasing processing time for applications

   - C) Decreasing staff competency

   - D) Limiting the understanding of insurance requirements

7. Direct communication with insurance company representatives can facilitate:

 - A) More frequent application errors

 - B) Slower resolution of issues

 - C) Smoother communication and quicker issue resolution

 - D) Increased complexity in the enrollment process

8. One way to ensure accuracy in the enrollment application is to:

 - A) Submit without reviewing

 - B) Use outdated information

 - C) Double-check applications for completeness and accuracy

 - D) Fill out applications randomly

9. Continuous education for enrollment staff is important due to:

 - A) The static nature of healthcare regulations

 - B) Decreased complexity in insurance policies

 - C) Frequent changes in healthcare regulations and insurance policies

 - D) The desire to reduce staff knowledge

10. A proactive approach to overcoming enrollment challenges includes all except:

   - A) Waiting for insurers to contact you first

   - B) Thorough preparation and research

   - C) Utilizing technology for application tracking

   - D) Seeking professional assistance when necessary

Answers

1. B) Provider enrollment with insurance companies

2. B) To allow providers to bill insurance companies for services rendered

3. C) Varying requirements across different insurers

4. A) Ignoring communications from insurance companies

5. B) Organizing and tracking the application process

6. A) Keeping up with regulatory changes and documentation practices

7. C) Smoother communication and quicker issue resolution

8. C) Double-check applications for completeness and accuracy

9. C) Frequent changes in healthcare regulations and insurance policies

10. A) Waiting for insurers to contact you first

These questions and answers are designed to reinforce the critical aspects of navigating the credentialing and provider enrollment processes, highlighting key strategies for addressing challenges and ensuring successful enrollment in insurance networks.

Chapter 13: International Credentialing Standards

13.1. Understanding Global Credentialing Practices

Navigating Credentialing Across Borders

In the increasingly globalized world of healthcare, understanding and navigating international credentialing practices is essential for healthcare organizations and providers who operate across borders or collaborate on an international scale. Credentialing standards vary significantly from country to country, reflecting differences in healthcare systems, regulatory environments, and professional qualifications. A comprehensive understanding of these practices ensures that healthcare providers meet the requisite standards of care and competence, regardless of location.

Key Aspects of International Credentialing

- **Variability in Standards:** Credentialing standards can vary widely, with each country having its own set of regulations, accreditation bodies, and certification requirements for healthcare providers.

- **Recognition of Foreign Qualifications:** One of the major challenges in international credentialing is the recognition of qualifications and certifications obtained in other countries. Processes for evaluating and recognizing foreign credentials are crucial for facilitating cross-border practice.

- **Regulatory Bodies and Professional Associations:** Many countries have specific regulatory bodies and professional associations responsible for overseeing credentialing processes. Understanding the role and requirements of these entities is key to successful credentialing.

- **Accreditation Systems:** International accreditation organizations, such as the Joint Commission International (JCI), provide standards and accreditation for healthcare organizations worldwide, ensuring a level of consistency in quality and safety standards.

Strategies for Navigating International Credentialing

- **Research and Preparation:** Comprehensive research into the credentialing requirements of the target country is essential. This may involve consulting with local regulatory bodies, professional associations, and international accreditation organizations.

- **Collaboration with Local Entities:** Establishing collaborations with local healthcare organizations, universities, and regulatory bodies can provide valuable insights and assistance in navigating the credentialing process.

- **Use of Credential Evaluation Services:** Specialized services can evaluate foreign credentials to determine their equivalence to local qualifications. These services can be invaluable in facilitating the recognition of qualifications across borders.

- **Adherence to International Accreditation Standards:** Seeking accreditation from recognized international bodies can help healthcare organizations meet global standards, facilitating the acceptance of their credentialing processes.

Challenges in International Credentialing

- **Complexity and Time-Consumption:** The complexity of international credentialing processes and the time required to navigate them can be significant, requiring careful planning and resources.

- **Legal and Ethical Considerations:** Navigating the legal frameworks governing healthcare practice in different countries, as well as ensuring ethical recruitment and practice standards, poses challenges.

- **Cultural and Language Barriers:** Cultural differences and language barriers can complicate the credentialing process, requiring additional considerations for training and adaptation.

Conclusion

Understanding global credentialing practices is crucial for ensuring the mobility of healthcare providers and the delivery of high-quality care in an international context. By navigating the variability in standards, leveraging local collaborations, and adhering to international accreditation, healthcare organizations can overcome the challenges associated with credentialing across borders. As the demand for global healthcare collaboration grows, so does the importance of efficient and effective international credentialing practices, underscoring the need for continuous learning, adaptation, and global cooperation in the healthcare sector.

13.2. Comparing U.S. and International Credentialing Processes

Navigating the Complex Landscape of Global Healthcare Credentialing

The credentialing process for healthcare providers varies significantly across the globe, influenced by each country's healthcare system, regulatory environment, and professional standards. Understanding the differences and similarities between U.S. and international credentialing processes is crucial for healthcare organizations operating in multiple countries, as well as for providers who seek to practice globally.

Key Differences Between U.S. and International Credentialing

- **Regulatory Environment:** The U.S. healthcare system is characterized by a complex regulatory environment with specific standards set by federal and state laws, as well as by various accrediting bodies. In contrast, other countries may have a more centralized healthcare system with credentialing standards and processes governed by national health ministries or professional regulatory organizations.

- **Credentialing Criteria:** While the core criteria for credentialing, such as verifying education, training, licensure, and work history, are generally consistent worldwide, the specific requirements and the emphasis placed on certain criteria can vary. For instance, some countries place a greater emphasis on in-country training and examinations, whereas others may readily accept international qualifications with specific equivalency assessments.

- **Credentialing Bodies:** In the U.S., credentialing is often conducted by individual healthcare organizations, managed care organizations, or credentialing verification organizations (CVOs). Internationally, credentialing may be more centralized, with national health services or professional councils playing a significant role in the credentialing of all healthcare providers within the country.

- **Primary Source Verification (PSV):** PSV is a critical component of the credentialing process, ensuring the accuracy of a provider's credentials directly from the issuing source. The process and extent of PSV can differ, with some countries having national databases that simplify verification, while others rely on more manual, paper-based processes.

- **Technology Integration:** The U.S. has seen significant adoption of technology in credentialing processes, with electronic health records (EHRs) and credentialing software becoming standard. Other countries may be at different stages of technology integration, affecting the efficiency and transparency of the credentialing process.

Similarities in Credentialing Processes

Despite these differences, there are fundamental similarities in the goal and importance of credentialing worldwide:

- **Ensuring Quality and Safety:** The primary aim of credentialing in any country is to ensure that healthcare providers meet the required standards of competence and professionalism to deliver safe and effective patient care.

- **Continuous Monitoring:** Most credentialing processes involve not only initial verification but also continuous monitoring of providers' credentials and performance to maintain high standards of care.

- **Adaptation to Changes:** Credentialing processes globally are subject to continuous updates and improvements to adapt to changes in healthcare delivery, technology, and regulations.

Implications for Global Practice

For healthcare providers seeking to practice in different countries, understanding the specific credentialing requirements and processes of each country is essential. Similarly, healthcare organizations operating internationally must navigate these diverse credentialing landscapes effectively to ensure compliance and maintain high standards of care.

Conclusion

Comparing U.S. and international credentialing processes reveals both unique challenges and universal goals in ensuring healthcare quality and safety. As healthcare becomes increasingly globalized, understanding these differences and similarities becomes crucial for providers and organizations aiming to deliver high-quality care across borders.

13.3. Working with International Graduates

Facilitating Integration into Diverse Healthcare Systems

Working with international graduates in healthcare settings presents unique challenges and opportunities for credentialing bodies, healthcare organizations, and the graduates themselves. These individuals, who have obtained their medical or healthcare qualifications from institutions outside the country where they intend to practice, must navigate a complex process of validation and adaptation. The goal is to ensure their credentials are recognized and that they can effectively contribute to the healthcare system while maintaining high standards of patient care.

Key Considerations for Credentialing International Graduates

- **Verification of International Credentials:** The first step involves the thorough verification of the graduate's qualifications, including degrees, licenses, and clinical training, from the original issuing institutions. This process often requires coordination with international credentialing services and may involve translation and equivalency evaluations to ensure compliance with local standards.

- **Understanding Regulatory Requirements:** International graduates must meet specific regulatory requirements that vary by country and sometimes by region within countries. These can include passing licensing examinations, completing additional training or residency programs, and demonstrating language proficiency.

- **Cultural and Systemic Adaptation:** Beyond verifying credentials and meeting regulatory requirements, international graduates often face the challenge of adapting to a new healthcare system, with its unique protocols, practices, and cultural nuances. Providing support for this adaptation process is crucial for their successful integration and for ensuring quality patient care.

Strategies for Supporting International Graduates

- **Orientation and Mentorship Programs:** Healthcare organizations can facilitate the integration of international graduates by offering comprehensive orientation programs that introduce them to the local healthcare system, practices, and culture. Mentorship by experienced professionals can provide additional support and guidance.

- **Continuing Education and Training:** Offering targeted continuing education and training opportunities can help international graduates fill any gaps in their knowledge or skills relative to local standards and practices. This can include updates on the latest clinical guidelines, technology training, and communication skills development.

- **Collaboration with Educational Institutions:** Building partnerships with educational institutions that have expertise in international medical education can provide valuable resources for credentialing and training international graduates.

- **Promoting Diversity and Inclusion:** Creating an inclusive environment that values the diverse backgrounds and perspectives of international graduates can enhance teamwork, innovation, and patient care. This includes addressing any biases and fostering a culture of respect and collaboration.

Challenges and Opportunities

- **Navigating Regulatory Differences:** The diversity of regulatory environments across countries can complicate the credentialing process for international graduates. Clear communication and guidance from credentialing bodies are essential.

- **Language and Communication Barriers:** Overcoming language barriers is not only about fluency but also understanding medical terminology and effective communication with patients and colleagues in the local context.

- **Recognition of International Experience:** While international graduates bring valuable perspectives and experiences, ensuring that these are recognized and utilized within the new healthcare setting is important for both the graduates and the organizations they join.

Conclusion

Working with international graduates requires a multifaceted approach from credentialing bodies and healthcare organizations, focusing on thorough credential verification, regulatory compliance, and support for cultural and systemic adaptation. By effectively addressing these considerations, the healthcare sector can harness the full potential of international graduates, enhancing the diversity, capacity, and quality of healthcare services.

13.4. Exercise: 10 MCQs with Answers at the End

Creating a set of 10 multiple-choice questions (MCQs) with answers at the end provides a structured way to review and reinforce the concepts discussed in Chapter 13, focusing on "International Credentialing Standards," particularly around understanding global credentialing practices, comparing U.S. and international processes, and working with international graduates. Here are the MCQs designed to encapsulate the key learnings:

Multiple Choice Questions

1. The primary aim of credentialing in any country is to:

   - A) Increase paperwork for healthcare providers.

   - B) Ensure healthcare providers meet required standards of competence.

   - C) Limit the number of healthcare providers in the market.

   - D) Standardize healthcare education globally.

2. A significant difference between U.S. and international credentialing processes is:

   - A) The use of technology in the U.S.

   - B) The focus on patient care in the U.S.

   - C) The regulatory environment and credentialing bodies.

   - D) The requirement for healthcare providers to have credentials.

3. An essential step for international graduates seeking to practice in a new country is:

   - A) Ignoring local regulatory requirements.

   - B) Verification of their international credentials.

   - C) Limiting their practice to areas they are familiar with.

   - D) Avoiding participation in orientation programs.

4. The process that allows healthcare providers to bill insurance companies for their services is called:

- A) Credentialing.

- B) Licensing.

- C) Enrollment.

- D) Certification.

5. Challenges for international graduates in adapting to a new healthcare system include all EXCEPT:

- A) Navigating a less complex regulatory environment.

- B) Cultural and systemic adaptation.

- C) Language and communication barriers.

- D) Understanding new protocols and practices.

6. Which strategy is NOT used to support the integration of international graduates?

- A) Providing comprehensive orientation programs.

- B) Encouraging isolation from local healthcare professionals.

- C) Offering continuing education and training opportunities.

- D) Promoting diversity and inclusion in the workplace.

7. Continuous professional development for international graduates is important due to:

- A) The static nature of healthcare standards.

- B) The lack of available resources for learning.

- C) Frequent changes in healthcare regulations and practices.

- D) Their inherent knowledge of all international healthcare systems.

8. The verification of a provider's qualifications from the original issuing source is known as:

- A) Primary Source Verification (PSV).

- B) Secondary Source Verification (SSV).

- C) Tertiary Education Verification (TEV).

- D) Credentialing Source Verification (CSV).

9. An effective way to overcome language barriers for international graduates is:

- A) Avoiding interactions with patients.

- B) Using medical jargon as much as possible.

- C) Providing language training and medical terminology support.

- D) Ignoring feedback on communication skills.

10. Regulatory and policy changes in healthcare:

   - A) Have little impact on the credentialing process.

   - B) Are typically uniform across different countries.

   - C) Can complicate the enrollment process for providers.

   - D) Reduce the need for continuous education.

Answers

1. B) Ensure healthcare providers meet required standards of competence.

2. C) The regulatory environment and credentialing bodies.

3. B) Verification of their international credentials.

4. C) Enrollment.

5. A) Navigating a less complex regulatory environment.

6. B) Encouraging isolation from local healthcare professionals.

7. C) Frequent changes in healthcare regulations and practices.

8. A) Primary Source Verification (PSV).

9. C) Providing language training and medical terminology support.

10. C) Can complicate the enrollment process for providers.

These questions and answers are designed to highlight the critical aspects of international credentialing standards, the challenges faced by international graduates, and the strategies for successful integration into new healthcare systems.

Chapter 14: Leadership and Management in Credentialing

14.1. Leading a Credentialing Team

Cultivating Effective Leadership in the Credentialing Process

Leading a credentialing team involves more than just overseeing the verification of qualifications and managing paperwork. It requires a strategic vision, effective communication, and a commitment to fostering a team environment where quality, efficiency, and continuous improvement are valued. Effective leadership in credentialing ensures that healthcare providers are qualified to deliver high-quality care, thereby protecting patients and supporting the organization's reputation and operational success.

Key Aspects of Effective Leadership in Credentialing

- **Vision and Strategy:** Leaders should have a clear vision for the credentialing process, understanding its critical role in healthcare delivery. This vision should be translated into a strategic plan that aligns with the organization's goals, addressing challenges and leveraging opportunities for improvement.

- **Communication and Collaboration:** Open, transparent communication is essential for keeping team members informed, engaged, and motivated. Leaders should facilitate collaboration within the team and with other departments, such as human resources, legal, and clinical departments, to streamline the credentialing process and resolve issues efficiently.

- **Professional Development:** Investing in the professional development of credentialing staff is crucial. This can include training on new technologies, updates on healthcare regulations, and best practices in credentialing. Encouraging certification in credentialing specialties can also enhance the team's expertise and credibility.

- **Performance Management:** Implementing robust performance management practices helps in setting clear expectations, monitoring progress, and providing feedback. Recognizing achievements and addressing areas for improvement contribute to a culture of excellence.

- **Adaptability and Problem-Solving:** Credentialing leaders must be adaptable, ready to face the ever-changing landscape of healthcare regulations, technology, and best practices. They should foster a problem-solving mindset within the team, encouraging innovative solutions to challenges.

Strategies for Leading a Credentialing Team

- **Foster a Positive Team Environment:** Create a supportive team environment that values diversity, encourages open dialogue, and recognizes individual and team contributions. This approach promotes engagement and job satisfaction.

- **Leverage Technology:** Stay informed about advancements in credentialing software and digital solutions that can enhance efficiency and accuracy. Leading the adoption of these technologies can significantly impact the team's performance.

- **Engage in Continuous Improvement:** Regularly review and assess the credentialing process for areas of improvement. Engaging the team in this process encourages a culture of continuous improvement and operational excellence.

- **Ensure Compliance and Quality:** Maintain a thorough understanding of compliance requirements and quality standards relevant to credentialing. Leading by example in upholding these standards sets the tone for the team's approach to their work.

Challenges in Leading a Credentialing Team

- **Managing Workload and Stress:** The credentialing process can be high-pressure and time-sensitive, leading to stress and burnout. Effective leaders must manage workloads, set realistic deadlines, and provide support to mitigate these issues.

- **Navigating Organizational Change:** Changes in healthcare delivery models, regulatory environments, and organizational structures can impact the credentialing process. Leaders must navigate these changes effectively, guiding their teams through transitions with minimal disruption.

Conclusion

Leading a credentialing team requires a balance of strategic vision, effective communication, and a focus on professional development and operational excellence. By cultivating these leadership qualities and strategies, credentialing leaders can ensure their teams are well-equipped to manage the complexities of the credentialing process, thereby contributing to the delivery of safe, high-quality healthcare services.

14.2. Project Management Skills

Essential for Effective Credentialing Operations

Project management skills are crucial for leading and executing credentialing processes efficiently. Credentialing, inherently project-based with its distinct phases, deadlines, and deliverables, requires a structured approach to ensure that healthcare providers are credentialed accurately and timely. Effective project management within credentialing can significantly impact healthcare organizations' operational efficiency, provider satisfaction, and patient care quality.

Key Project Management Skills in Credentialing

- **Planning and Organization:** This involves developing a comprehensive plan that outlines the credentialing process, including timelines, responsibilities, and resources needed. Effective planning ensures that every phase of credentialing is executed systematically, minimizing delays and errors.

- **Communication:** Clear, consistent communication with all stakeholders involved in the credentialing process is vital. This includes credentialing team members, healthcare providers, insurance companies, and regulatory bodies. Effective communication ensures that information is shared accurately and promptly, facilitating a smoother credentialing process.

- **Risk Management:** Identifying potential risks and challenges that could impede the credentialing process, such as delays in obtaining necessary documentation or changes in regulatory requirements, and developing strategies to mitigate these risks.

- **Team Leadership and Motivation:** Leading a credentialing team requires not only directing team efforts towards common goals but also motivating team members, providing support, and fostering a collaborative work environment.

- **Problem-Solving:** The ability to quickly and effectively resolve issues that arise during the credentialing process, from discrepancies in documentation to delays in verification, is crucial. Problem-solving skills ensure that credentialing operations proceed without significant disruptions.

- **Adaptability and Flexibility:** Credentialing environments are dynamic, with frequent changes in regulations, healthcare standards, and provider information. Being adaptable and flexible allows project managers to adjust plans and processes in response to these changes.

- **Time Management:** Efficiently managing the time of both the credentialing team and the process itself ensures that credentialing is completed within established deadlines, enabling providers to begin delivering care as soon as possible.

- **Technology Proficiency:** Understanding and leveraging technology, such as credentialing software and databases, can enhance the efficiency and accuracy of the credentialing process.

Implementing Effective Project Management Practices

- **Use of Project Management Tools:** Utilizing project management software or tools can help in tracking progress, managing deadlines, and ensuring that all tasks are completed as scheduled.

- **Regular Progress Reviews:** Conducting regular meetings or reviews to assess the progress of the credentialing process, identify any issues, and adjust plans as necessary.

- **Stakeholder Engagement:** Actively involving stakeholders in the planning and execution phases of credentialing projects ensures that their needs and concerns are addressed, and they are committed to the process.

- **Continuous Improvement:** Implementing a continuous improvement approach, where feedback is collected and analyzed to make ongoing enhancements to the credentialing process.

Conclusion

Project management skills are indispensable in the realm of credentialing, providing the framework and tools necessary to navigate the complexities of the process efficiently. By applying these skills, credentialing leaders can ensure that their teams are effective, processes are streamlined, and the organization can meet its goal of delivering high-quality patient care through a competent and credentialed provider network.

14.3. Strategic Planning for Credentialing Operations

Aligning Credentialing Processes with Organizational Goals

Strategic planning in credentialing operations involves setting long-term goals and designing a roadmap to achieve them, aligning the credentialing process with the broader objectives of the healthcare organization. This strategic approach not only optimizes the credentialing process but also ensures it supports the delivery of high-quality patient care, compliance with regulatory standards, and the organization's financial health.

Components of Strategic Planning in Credentialing

- **Assessment of Current Operations:** A thorough analysis of the existing credentialing process, identifying strengths, weaknesses, opportunities for improvement, and challenges. This includes evaluating the efficiency of processes, technology utilization, team skills, and compliance rates.

- **Setting Strategic Goals:** Based on the assessment, define clear, measurable goals for the credentialing operations that align with the organization's mission and objectives. Goals might include reducing credentialing times, improving provider satisfaction, enhancing compliance with regulatory standards, or implementing new technologies.

- **Developing Action Plans:** For each strategic goal, develop detailed action plans that outline the steps needed to achieve the goal, assign responsibilities, set timelines, and identify required resources.

- **Stakeholder Engagement:** Engaging key stakeholders, including credentialing staff, healthcare providers, management, and external partners, in the strategic planning process ensures buy-in and support for the strategic initiatives.

- **Monitoring and Evaluation:** Establish metrics and KPIs (Key Performance Indicators) to monitor progress towards the strategic goals and evaluate the effectiveness of the implemented strategies. Regular reviews allow for adjustments to the plan as needed.

Strategies for Successful Strategic Planning

- **Leverage Technology:** Assess and integrate advanced credentialing technologies and systems to streamline processes, enhance accuracy, and improve efficiency.

- **Focus on Training and Development:** Invest in continuous training and professional development opportunities for the credentialing team to ensure they possess the skills needed to meet evolving challenges and standards.

- **Promote Collaboration:** Foster a culture of collaboration and communication within the credentialing team and across departments to ensure alignment and support for strategic goals.

- **Adapt to Regulatory Changes:** Stay informed about changes in healthcare regulations and standards to ensure that credentialing processes remain compliant and are proactively adjusted to meet new requirements.

- **Prioritize Provider Relations:** Develop strategies to enhance communication and support for healthcare providers throughout the credentialing process, improving their experience and satisfaction.

Challenges in Strategic Planning for Credentialing

- **Rapidly Changing Healthcare Landscape:** Navigating the fast-paced changes in healthcare regulations, technologies, and practices can make it challenging to maintain a strategic focus.

- **Resource Constraints:** Limited resources, including budget, staff, and time, can impact the ability to implement strategic initiatives.

- **Resistance to Change:** Implementing new processes or technologies may encounter resistance from staff or providers accustomed to existing procedures.

Overcoming Challenges

- **Flexibility and Adaptability:** Being flexible and open to adjusting strategic plans in response to new information or changing circumstances is crucial.

- **Effective Communication:** Clear, transparent communication about the benefits of strategic initiatives and changes can help overcome resistance and garner support.

- **Strategic Resource Allocation:** Carefully prioritize initiatives based on their potential impact and allocate resources strategically to ensure the most critical areas are addressed first.

Conclusion

Strategic planning for credentialing operations is essential for aligning credentialing processes with the goals of the healthcare organization and ensuring they contribute effectively to the provision of high-quality patient care. Through careful planning, stakeholder engagement, and continuous evaluation, healthcare organizations can optimize their credentialing operations to meet the challenges of the modern healthcare landscape.

14.4. Exercise: 10 MCQs with Answers at the End

Creating a set of 10 multiple-choice questions (MCQs) with answers at the end offers a way to review and reinforce the concepts discussed in Chapter 14, focusing on "Leadership and Management in Credentialing," particularly around leading a credentialing team, project management skills, and strategic planning for credentialing operations. Here are the MCQs designed to encapsulate the key learnings:

Multiple Choice Questions

1. Effective leadership in a credentialing team requires:

   - A) Ignoring team feedback.

   - B) Micromanaging team members.

   - C) Motivating and guiding the team towards common goals.

   - D) Avoiding decision-making.

2. A crucial project management skill in credentialing is:

   - A) Planning and organization.

   - B) Procrastination.

   - C) Ignoring risks.

   - D) Limiting communication with stakeholders.

3. The first step in strategic planning for credentialing operations is:

   - A) Setting unrealistic goals.

   - B) Assessment of current operations.

   - C) Decreasing team collaboration.

   - D) Implementing changes without analysis.

4. A significant challenge in leading credentialing operations is:

   - A) Excessive resources.

   - B) Lack of changes in healthcare regulations.

   - C) Navigating the complex regulatory environment.

   - D) Having too few tasks to manage.

5. Effective communication in a credentialing team does NOT involve:

   - A) Sharing information transparently.

   - B) Encouraging open dialogue.

   - C) Withholding important updates from the team.

   - D) Regular team meetings.

6. Risk management in credentialing processes involves:

   - A) Ignoring potential issues until they become critical.

- B) Identifying potential risks and developing strategies to mitigate them.

   - C) Avoiding new projects to minimize risks.

   - D) Blaming external factors for any problems.

7. When implementing strategic planning in credentialing, it's important to:

   - A) Avoid engaging stakeholders in the process.

   - B) Develop detailed action plans for each goal.

   - C) Set goals without considering organizational objectives.

   - D) Assume that the initial plan will not require adjustments.

8. Adapting to regulatory changes in credentialing requires:

   - A) Sticking strictly to old procedures.

   - B) Waiting for external mandates before making any changes.

   - C) Continuous education and flexibility.

   - D) Isolating the credentialing department from the rest of the organization.

9. Monitoring and evaluation of credentialing processes should:

   - A) Be conducted only when issues arise.

   - B) Use clear metrics and KPIs to assess progress.

   - C) Ignore feedback from healthcare providers.

   - D) Focus solely on the number of credentialed providers.

10. A strategy to overcome resistance to change in credentialing operations is to:

   - A) Penalize dissenters.

   - B) Communicate the benefits of strategic initiatives clearly.

   - C) Implement changes secretly.

   - D) Avoid discussing changes with the team.

Answers

1. C) Motivating and guiding the team towards common goals.

2. A) Planning and organization.

3. B) Assessment of current operations.

4. C) Navigating the complex regulatory environment.

5. C) Withholding important updates from the team.

6. B) Identifying potential risks and developing strategies to mitigate them.

7. B) Develop detailed action plans for each goal.

8. C) Continuous education and flexibility.

9. B) Use clear metrics and KPIs to assess progress.

10. B) Communicate the benefits of strategic initiatives clearly.

These questions and answers are designed to highlight the importance of leadership, project management, and strategic planning in effectively managing credentialing operations within healthcare organizations.

Chapter 15: Future Trends in Medical Credentialing

15.1. Innovations in Credentialing Technology

Embracing Technological Advancements for Streamlined Processes

The landscape of medical credentialing is rapidly evolving, driven by technological innovations that promise to streamline processes, enhance accuracy, and improve efficiency. As healthcare organizations strive to meet the growing demands for quality care, the adoption of advanced technologies in credentialing becomes not just beneficial but essential. These innovations are transforming traditional credentialing methods, offering new ways to verify provider qualifications, manage data, and ensure compliance with regulatory standards.

Key Technological Innovations in Credentialing

- **Blockchain Technology:** Blockchain offers a secure, immutable ledger for storing credentialing information, enabling instant verification of credentials without the need for third-party verification agencies. This technology can significantly reduce the time and cost associated with credentialing processes while enhancing data security and integrity.

- **Artificial Intelligence (AI) and Machine Learning:** AI and machine learning algorithms can automate the verification of credentials, flag discrepancies, and predict potential credentialing issues before they arise. These technologies can also assist in maintaining up-to-date provider data, reducing manual errors, and streamlining credentialing workflows.

- **Credentialing Databases and Cloud-Based Platforms:** Cloud-based credentialing platforms allow for the centralized management of provider credentials, facilitating easy access, updates, and sharing of information across departments and healthcare facilities. These platforms often feature automated reminders for credential renewals, expirations, and compliance requirements, ensuring that provider credentials are always current.

- **Digital Credentials and E-Badging:** The digitalization of credentials and the use of electronic badges (e-badges) make it easier for providers to share their qualifications with multiple organizations securely. E-badging can also support the quick identification of providers' specialties, training, and competencies, facilitating better matching of provider skills with patient care needs.

- **Telemedicine Credentialing Modules:** As telemedicine continues to grow, credentialing solutions are being developed to address the unique challenges of credentialing telehealth providers. These modules are designed to ensure that providers meet all regulatory and licensure requirements for delivering remote care across state lines.

Challenges and Considerations

While these technological innovations offer significant advantages, they also present challenges that healthcare organizations must navigate:

- **Data Privacy and Security:** The adoption of new technologies must be accompanied by stringent data protection measures to safeguard sensitive provider information against breaches and cyber threats.

- **Interoperability:** Ensuring that new credentialing technologies can integrate seamlessly with existing healthcare IT systems and databases is crucial for their effective implementation.

- **Regulatory Compliance:** Technologies must be compliant with healthcare regulations, including those related to data privacy, telehealth, and interstate licensure.

- **Adoption and Training:** Successfully implementing new technologies requires adequate training for credentialing staff and providers to adapt to new systems and processes.

The Future of Credentialing Technology

The future of medical credentialing will likely see continued innovation, with technologies becoming more sophisticated and integrated into the broader healthcare ecosystem. As these technologies evolve, they will enable healthcare organizations to credential providers more quickly, accurately, and with greater transparency, ultimately contributing to the delivery of safer, higher-quality care.

Conclusion

Innovations in credentialing technology are set to transform the credentialing landscape, offering solutions to longstanding challenges and opening new possibilities for efficiency and accuracy. By staying informed about and adopting these technological advancements, healthcare organizations can enhance their credentialing processes, ensuring that they are well-equipped to meet the demands of modern healthcare delivery.

15.2. The Impact of Healthcare Reforms

Navigating Changes in Credentialing Amidst Policy Shifts

Healthcare reforms, whether at the national, regional, or global level, significantly impact various aspects of healthcare delivery, including the credentialing process. These reforms often aim to improve access to care, enhance the quality of services, and ensure patient safety, directly influencing credentialing standards, procedures, and requirements. Understanding the implications of these reforms is crucial for healthcare organizations and credentialing bodies to adapt their practices accordingly.

Key Areas of Impact

- **Expanded Access to Care:** Reforms that expand access to healthcare often require an increase in the healthcare workforce. This can lead to changes in credentialing processes to expedite the inclusion of more providers in the system, sometimes necessitating temporary or emergency credentialing procedures during public health emergencies.

- **Quality and Safety Standards:** Reforms focusing on improving healthcare quality and patient safety may introduce new credentialing standards and continuous quality improvement measures. Healthcare organizations may need to enhance their credentialing processes to comply with these heightened standards, ensuring that all providers meet the new criteria.

- **Telehealth and Cross-State Licensure:** With the expansion of telehealth services, particularly highlighted during the COVID-19 pandemic, reforms may address cross-state licensure and telehealth credentialing. These changes require credentialing processes to adapt to new models of care delivery, ensuring providers are credentialed to offer telehealth services across state lines or even internationally.

- **Interoperability and Data Sharing:** Reforms that promote interoperability and data sharing among healthcare systems can impact credentialing by facilitating easier access to provider credentials and histories. Credentialing bodies may need to integrate new technologies or join shared credentialing networks to streamline verification and reduce duplicative efforts.

- **Regulatory Compliance:** Healthcare reforms often come with new regulations or modifications to existing ones. Credentialing processes must remain compliant with these changes, necessitating regular reviews and updates to policies, procedures, and documentation requirements.

Strategies for Adapting to Healthcare Reforms

- **Continuous Monitoring:** Stay informed about ongoing and proposed healthcare reforms and assess their potential impact on credentialing processes. This proactive approach allows for timely adjustments and compliance.

- **Stakeholder Engagement:** Engage with key stakeholders, including healthcare providers, regulatory bodies, and accreditation organizations, to understand the implications of reforms and collaborate on effective responses.

- **Training and Education:** Provide regular training for credentialing staff on new regulations, standards, and technologies. Ensuring that staff are well-informed and equipped to handle changes is essential for maintaining the integrity of the credentialing process.

- **Technology Integration:** Leverage technology to enhance flexibility and efficiency in credentialing processes. Adopting credentialing software that can easily be updated to reflect new standards or requirements can mitigate the impact of reforms.

- **Policy and Procedure Updates:** Regularly review and update credentialing policies and procedures to ensure alignment with new healthcare regulations and standards. Clear documentation and communication of these changes to all involved parties are crucial.

Conclusion

Healthcare reforms present both challenges and opportunities for the credentialing process. By understanding the impact of these reforms and adopting strategies to adapt, healthcare organizations and credentialing bodies can ensure that their processes remain effective, compliant, and aligned with the goals of improving healthcare access, quality, and patient safety. The ability to navigate these changes successfully is integral to supporting the evolving landscape of healthcare delivery.

15.3. Preparing for the Future of Credentialing

Adapting to Evolving Healthcare Landscapes

The future of medical credentialing is poised for significant evolution, driven by advancements in technology, changing healthcare delivery models, and ongoing regulatory reforms. Healthcare organizations and credentialing bodies must anticipate and prepare for these changes to ensure the credentialing process remains efficient, effective, and aligned with the overarching goals of improving patient care and safety. Here are key strategies for navigating the future of credentialing:

Embrace Technological Advancements

- **Invest in Credentialing Software:** Adopt and invest in comprehensive credentialing software solutions that offer automation, data analytics, and integration capabilities. This technology can streamline the credentialing process, reduce manual errors, and improve overall efficiency.

- **Explore Blockchain Applications:** Consider the potential of blockchain technology for secure, immutable storage and sharing of credentialing information. Blockchain can facilitate instant verification of credentials across organizations, enhancing transparency and trust.

- **Leverage Artificial Intelligence (AI):** Utilize AI and machine learning to automate routine tasks, such as data entry and verification, and to analyze patterns that could predict credentialing bottlenecks or compliance risks.

Stay Informed and Adaptable to Regulatory Changes

- **Monitor Healthcare Reforms:** Regularly review and assess the impact of healthcare reforms on credentialing standards and processes. Being proactive in understanding these changes allows for timely adaptation and compliance.

- **Engage in Policy Discussions:** Participate in industry discussions and policy-making processes related to credentialing standards and healthcare delivery. This involvement can provide insights into future trends and regulatory shifts.

Enhance Training and Professional Development

- **Continuous Learning:** Encourage and facilitate continuous learning and professional development opportunities for credentialing staff. Keeping abreast of the latest trends, technologies, and best practices is crucial for adapting to the future landscape of credentialing.

- **Cross-Training:** Implement cross-training programs to develop a more versatile credentialing team capable of handling various aspects of the process, from primary source verification to compliance monitoring.

Promote Inter-organizational Collaboration

- **Build Networks and Partnerships:** Foster collaboration and networking with other healthcare organizations, credentialing bodies, and technology providers. Sharing knowledge, resources, and best practices can lead to more standardized and efficient credentialing processes across the industry.

- **Participate in Credentialing Consortia:** Engage in or form consortia that allow for shared credentialing services and mutual recognition of credentials. This approach can reduce duplication of efforts and accelerate the credentialing of providers across multiple organizations.

Prioritize Data Security and Privacy

- **Implement Robust Data Protection Measures:** As credentialing processes become more digitized, ensuring the security and privacy of provider data is paramount. Adopt stringent data protection policies and invest in cybersecurity measures to safeguard sensitive information.

Conclusion

Preparing for the future of credentialing requires a multifaceted approach that embraces innovation, prioritizes adaptability, and fosters collaboration. By staying informed about technological and regulatory developments, investing in staff training, and focusing on data security, healthcare organizations and credentialing bodies can navigate the evolving landscape effectively. These strategies will not only enhance the credentialing process but also contribute to the broader goal of delivering safe, high-quality healthcare in an ever-changing environment.

15.4. Exercise: 10 MCQs with Answers at the End

Creating a set of 10 multiple-choice questions (MCQs) with answers at the end offers a way to review and reinforce the concepts discussed in Chapter 15, focusing on "Future Trends in Medical Credentialing," particularly around innovations in credentialing technology, the impact of healthcare reforms, and preparing for the future of credentialing. Here are the MCQs designed to encapsulate the key learnings:

Multiple Choice Questions

1. Which technology is predicted to significantly reduce the time and cost associated with credentialing processes?

   - A) Blockchain technology

   - B) Fax machines

   - C) Postal mail

   - D) Typewriters

2. AI and machine learning in credentialing can automate:

   - A) The creation of more paperwork

   - B) Verification of credentials and prediction of issues

   - C) Manual data entry only

   - D) Decrease in data accuracy

3. The primary goal of adopting new technologies in credentialing is to:

  - A) Increase the complexity of processes

  - B) Streamline processes and enhance accuracy

  - C) Limit access to credentialing information

  - D) Slow down the verification process

4. Continuous monitoring and adaptation to healthcare reforms are crucial due to:

  - A) The static nature of healthcare regulations

  - B) Decreasing legal requirements

  - C) Frequent changes in healthcare regulations and practices

  - D) The unchanging landscape of healthcare delivery

5. A key strategy for navigating the future of credentialing includes:

  - A) Ignoring technological advancements

  - B) Staying informed about and adaptable to regulatory changes

  - C) Reducing training opportunities for credentialing staff

  - D) Isolating from industry discussions and policy-making processes

6. Effective project management in credentialing involves:

   - A) Avoiding setting clear timelines and responsibilities

   - B) Excluding stakeholders from the planning process

   - C) Planning and organization of the credentialing process

   - D) Maintaining outdated technology systems

7. Blockchain technology in credentialing primarily enhances:

   - A) Data insecurity and opacity

   - B) Time to complete credentialing due to manual verification

   - C) Data security and transparency

   - D) Paper-based recordkeeping

8. Strategic planning for credentialing operations should:

   - A) Disregard organizational goals and objectives

   - B) Exclude technology integration

   - C) Align with the organization's mission and objectives

   - D) Avoid engaging key stakeholders in the process

9. Preparing for the future of credentialing necessitates:

   - A) Decreasing adaptability to changes

   - B) Embracing technological advancements

   - C) Sole reliance on traditional credentialing methods

- D) Ignoring the development of staff skills

10. The impact of healthcare reforms on credentialing processes underscores the need for:

   - A) Reduced compliance with regulatory standards

   - B) Continuous monitoring and adaptability

   - C) Ignoring reforms until mandated by law

   - D) Elimination of digital credentialing tools

Answers

1. A) Blockchain technology

2. B) Verification of credentials and prediction of issues

3. B) Streamline processes and enhance accuracy

4. C) Frequent changes in healthcare regulations and practices

5. B) Staying informed about and adaptable to regulatory changes

6. C) Planning and organization of the credentialing process

7. C) Data security and transparency

8. C) Align with the organization's mission and objectives

9. B) Embracing technological advancements

10. B) Continuous monitoring and adaptability

These questions and answers are designed to highlight the importance of innovations in technology, the need for adaptability in the face of healthcare reforms, and the strategies for preparing for the evolving future of medical credentialing.

Conclusion

As we conclude our exploration of the multifaceted world of medical credentialing, it's clear that this critical process plays a pivotal role in maintaining the standards of healthcare delivery. From the foundational practices of verifying qualifications to adapting to the latest innovations in technology and navigating the complexities of healthcare reforms, credentialing ensures that healthcare providers are competent, qualified, and capable of delivering high-quality care to patients.

The chapters covered offer a comprehensive view of the current state and future directions of credentialing, highlighting the importance of leadership, strategic planning, and the need for continuous adaptation to technological advancements and regulatory changes. The exercises provided, including multiple-choice questions, serve to reinforce the key concepts discussed, offering a structured way to review and assess understanding.

In preparing for the future of credentialing, healthcare organizations and credentialing bodies must remain vigilant and adaptable, embracing new technologies, fostering collaboration, and continuously improving processes to meet the evolving demands of healthcare delivery. By doing so, they can ensure that the credentialing process remains a robust safeguard for patient safety and care quality, supporting the overarching goal of improving health outcomes for all.

Thank you for engaging with this comprehensive overview of medical credentialing. It's our hope that the insights and strategies discussed will serve as valuable resources for those involved in the credentialing process, contributing to the ongoing enhancement of healthcare quality and patient safety in an ever-changing landscape.

*The best way to thank an author is
to
write a review.*